ALL CLEAR

Listening and Speaking

Helen Kalkstein Fragiadakis

THOMSON

HEINLE

Australia · Canada · Mexico · Singapore · Spain · United Kingdom · United States

THOMSON
HEINLE

All Clear 1
Listening and Speaking
Helen Kalkstein Fragiadakis

Publisher, Academic ESL: James W. Brown
Executive Editor, Dictionaries and Adult ESL: Sherrise Roehr
Director of Content Development: Anita Raducanu
Associate Development Editor: Katherine Carroll
Associate Development Editor: Jennifer Meldrum
Director of Product Marketing: Amy Mabley
Senior Field Marketing Manager: Donna Lee Kennedy
Associate Marketing Manager: Caitlin Driscoll

Senior Production Editor: Maryellen E. Killeen
Senior Print Buyer: Betsy Donaghey
Project Manager: Tunde Dewey
Composition: Parkwood Composition
Interior Design: Lori Stuart
Artist: Steve Haefele
Printer: Edwards Brothers

Printed in the United States of America.
1 2 3 4 5 6 7 8 9 10   09 08 07 06

For more information contact Thomson Heinle, 25 Thomson Place, Boston, MA 02210 USA, or visit our Internet site at elt.thomson.com

For permission to use material from this text or product, submit a request online at http://www.thomsonrights.com

Any additional questions about permissions can be submitted by email to thomsonrights@thomson.com

ISBN 10: 1-4130-1703-7
ISBN 13: 978-1-4130-1703-8
ISE ISBN 10: 1-4130-2097-6
ISE ISBN 13: 978-1-4130-2097-7

To my family, yesterday and today—

Acknowledgments

The original *All Clear* idioms text came out more than twenty years ago, and the additional two texts at higher and lower levels appeared years later. It was always my dream for these three texts to become a comprehensive listening and speaking series using idioms and other expressions as springboards for activities, and I have many people to thank for making this dream come true.

To Jim Brown, publisher, and Sherrise Roehr, executive editor, thank you for getting the ball rolling on this project. To Katie Carroll and Jennifer Meldrum, my developmental editors, thank you for your wonderful attention and detailed suggestions. To Maryellen Eschmann-Killeen, Tunde Dewey, and the rest of the production team, thank you for your enthusiasm, creativity, and wonderful work.

I would also like to express my gratitude to the many colleagues who over the years gave me extremely valuable feedback, which I incorporated into the new editions. I would especially like to thank Inocencia Dacumos, Rosemary Loughman, Helen Munch, Kathleen Pappert, Ellen Rosenfield, and Larry Statan.

A big thank you goes to my daughter Melissa, who for years has enthusiastically given me feedback to help make the language in *All Clear* dialogues as natural as possible. Thank you, Melissa, for using your wonderful sense of *what people really say* to answer such questions as "How would you say this?", "Would you ever say that?", "Does this sound natural?", and "What's another way to say. . . ?"

I would also like to thank my many students for their interest and insightful questions as I taught with the *All Clear* texts. While teaching, I jotted down their questions in the textbook margins. And then, while revising the texts, I used their questions as guides to improve the material.

Finally, I would like to thank Michael Lewis, who has put the lexical approach in the center stage of language acquisition. I wrote the first *All Clear* in the early 1980s, and ten years later it was a revelation to hear Lewis talk about the value of teaching "chunks" of language—collocations and fixed expressions. I have found that focusing on lexical items (many, but not all of them, idiomatic) in a natural dialogue can provide concrete material that can serve as a springboard for numerous activities in a listening/speaking class. Thank you, Michael Lewis, for bringing the lexical approach to the forefront of language teaching and learning.

Helen Kalkstein Fragiadakis
March, 2006

CONTENTS

CONTENTS

CONTENTS

CONTENTS

A Walk-Through Guide

All Clear 1—Listening and Speaking (intro level) is the first in this best-selling series of conversationally-oriented texts. High-frequency American English expressions such as *make friends,* and *eat out* are presented in meaningful contexts to develop speaking, listening, and pronunciation skills. This text is appropriate for high-beginner and intermediate level listening/speaking, pronunciation, and vocabulary courses.

- **Theme-based units** feature more contextualized listening activities.

- **Culture Note** boxes in every lesson apply the theme to the outside world and encourage discussion.

- **After You Listen** sections after each conversation increase comprehension.

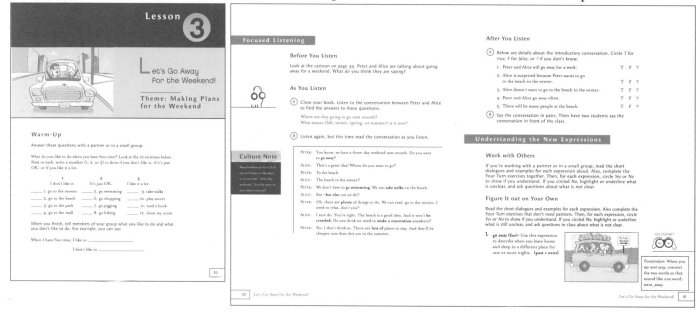

- **Your Turn** sections enhance comprehension by giving students the chance to personalize and connect expressions to their own lives and experiences.

- **Pronunciation** opportunities in every lesson allow students to practice conversation skills.

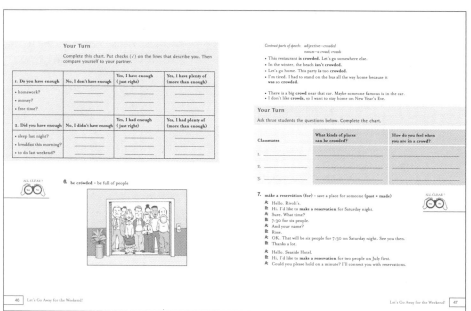

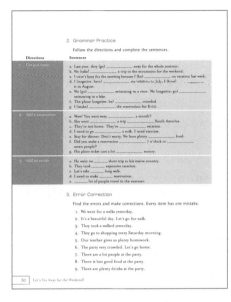

- **Grammar Practice** sections in every lesson teach students how to use expressions in complete, correct sentences.

- **Error Correction** sections provide editing practice.

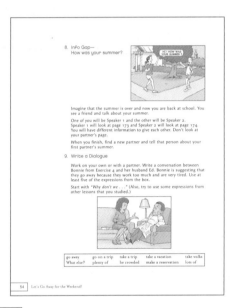

  - Opportunities for **role-playing, group work** and **delivering speeches** increase oral communication skills while meeting state standards.

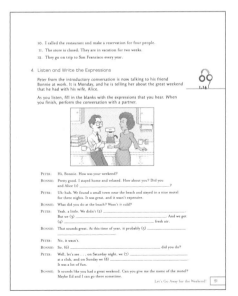

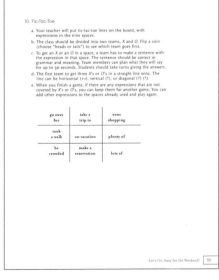

- More **communicative activities** emphasize the practical uses of expressions in everyday conversations.

All Clear 1— Listening and Speaking is the new edition of *All Clear! Intro.* Because the material in *All Clear 1* focuses on listening, speaking, and pronunciation in addition to vocabulary, this revised text would be appropriate in the following types of classes at the high-beginning and intermediate level: listening/speaking, vocabulary, and pronunciation.

It was in the early 1980s when I wrote the first *All Clear*, which focused on idioms, and it is refreshing today to see such great interest in teaching with a lexical approach. While the initial focus of each lesson in this text is on lexical chunks of language, students gain practice in all skill areas: listening, speaking, pronunciation, grammar, reading and writing.

All Clear 1 differs from *All Clear 2* and *3* in that this text does *not* teach expressions that are highly idiomatic. The focus here is instead on very common phrases and expressions needed by students at this level.

It is well-known that in listening/speaking classes, it can be difficult to give homework and test and grade students because of the nature of the many open-ended activities. The inclusion of vocabulary, in the form of phrases and expressions, brings in more concrete language material that can be easily assigned as homework and subsequently assessed.

All Clear 1

- exposes students to conversational situations that can serve as a basis for conversation practice, often with a cross-cultural focus.
- provides many structured and communicative activities for speaking, listening, grammar, writing, and pronunciation practice.
- teaches students to recognize and produce high-frequency phrases and expressions.
- contextualizes the study of pronunciation by integrating it with the study of expressions.

All Clear 1 starts with an icebreaker activity, and is then divided into eight lessons, four review sections, a pronunciation section, and twelve appendices.

Icebreaker

To get to know each other, students mill around and ask each other questions based on information taken from student questionnaires completed at the previous class meeting. A sample questionnaire and sample *Find Someone Who . . .* activity are provided. With the latter, you will need to decide whether to provide the *yes-no* questions or have your students construct them.

Lessons

The lessons integrate listening, speaking, pronunciation, grammar, and writing, while focusing on teaching common expressions. Throughout each lesson, students are given opportunities to be very active and involved learners. Varied activities and numerous visuals are designed to reach students with a range of learning styles.

It is possible to move through the text in random order. Each lesson is independent, except in one area: pronunciation. If you plan to make pronunciation a substantial component of your course, you might prefer to follow the lessons in order because the pronunciation points build upon one another. The pronunciation part of each lesson appears in a separate section towards the back of the text.

You might want to start with Lesson 1 because it has more detailed instructions than the other lessons.

Warm-Up

Students answer questions about their opinions or personal experience related to the lesson theme.

Focused Listening

Before You Listen: Students look at a cartoon and try to guess what the characters are saying.

As You Listen: Students listen to a conversation with their books closed, and then answer two general questions about the main idea. They listen again as they read the conversation.

After You Listen: To check their comprehension of details, students complete a short exercise.

Understanding the New Expressions

This section teaches the meanings, forms, and uses of expressions that appear in the introductory conversation.

- Meanings are revealed in explanations, mini-dialogues, and example sentences.
- Related expressions (those that are similar or opposite in appearance and/or meaning) are included.
- Grammar and pronunciation notes call students' attention to details about expressions. Notes about usage are also included.
- *Your Turn* activities make this section interactive. Students immediately have opportunities to work with each other and use the new expressions.
- One *Your Turn: Listening Challenge* per lesson provides an additional listening opportunity.
- Students evaluate their understanding of expressions by indicating whether or not the meanings are *all clear.*

Exercises

Students do exercises individually, in pairs, and in groups. When students work in groups, you might want to assign roles: leader, reporter, timekeeper, participant. Group leaders should make sure that students know each other's names, that everyone participates in a balanced way, and that the group stays on task and completes the activity at hand.

The ten exercises move from structured to communicative. (The exercises with an asterisk appear on the audio program.)

Focus on Form and Meaning

1. **Mini-Dialogues** (matching): In the mini-dialogues, students see the expressions in new contexts that help them understand the meanings of the expressions.*

2. **Grammar Practice**: Given specific directions to use certain parts of speech or change verb tenses, students focus on form.

3. **Error Correction**: Students continue to focus on form as they analyze sentences with errors.

4. **Listen and Write Expressions** (fill-in): As they listen, students insert expressions into a new conversation.

5. **Write Sentences**: In this less structured exercise, students have the opportunity to use the new expressions in individual sentences or dialogues.

6. **Dictation**: For more listening practice, students listen to a summary of the introductory conversation. Key words are provided to help with spelling.*

Focus on Communication

7. **Walk and Talk**: In this communicative exercise, students mill around and ask their classmates a variety of questions, some of which are based on the lesson theme, and some of which require the use of expressions. As a follow-up, students write their own or other students' responses to the questions.

8. The focus of this activity varies. Students have opportunities to conduct group surveys, participate in role plays, do an information gap activity, or take what they have learned to the outside world in a contact assignment.

9. **Write a Dialogue**: Given an illustration and a new context, students create dialogues with some of the expressions that they have studied.

10. **Games and Puzzles**: In word searches, unscrambling activities, and Tic-Tac-Toe games, students have fun using what they have learned.

At the end of each lesson, speech topics related to the lesson theme are suggested. In addition, individual students sit on the *Hot Seat* where they respond to questions from their classmates.

Review Sections

After every two lessons, a "Collocation Match-Up" exercise and a crossword puzzle provide students with opportunities for review.

Pronunciation Section

This section, which usually focuses on suprasegmentals (stress, intonation and rhythm), appears towards the back of the text. This allows the teacher to introduce this material if time allows and at whatever time point in a lesson it may be appropriate. The contexts of the pronunciation exercises come from each lesson, providing students with meaningful material for practice.

Appendices

- **Appendices A–D** provide necessary information for specific parts of lessons.
- **Appendices E–F** provide supplementary information that can be incorporated into instruction whenever you wish. You might want to introduce your students to Appendix E, Classroom Language, at the beginning of your course. And if you would like to focus on the pronunciation of vowels and consonants (not covered in the pronunciation section), you can refer to Appendix F.
- **Appendices G** and **H** relate to study skills. These appendices include information on how to create vocabulary cards and how to cluster and organize expressions as students learn them. **Appendices I** and **J** provide one verbal and visual way for students to assess their learning.
- **Appendices K** and **L** provide systems for documenting expressions that students hear and read outside of class.

Audio Program

The audio program uses natural speech to present the following from each lesson:

- Introductory Conversation
- Listening Challenge
- Exercise 1—Mini-Dialogues
- Exercise 4—Listen and Write the Expressions
- Exercise 6—Dictation
- Pronunciation

I hope that you and your students enjoy using *All Clear 1,* and I welcome your comments and suggestions.

Helen Kalkstein Fragiadakis
Contra Costa College
San Pablo, California

Dear Student,

Welcome to ***All Clear 1 Listening and Speaking.*** I hope that you have a good time using this book.

As a student of English, you know that you need to learn a lot of new vocabulary. In this book, you will learn a lot of vocabulary but you won't learn just words—you will learn groups of words called *expressions*.

Here are some example of expressions:

- take a walk
- go to bed
- be afraid of
- pick someone up

You will study what these expressions mean. You will also learn to pronounce them. And you will learn about using these expressions with the correct grammar. You will have a lot of listening and speaking practice, too.

When you use this book, you will talk a lot and have fun.
I wish you good luck, and I hope that you find this book to be *all clear.*

Sincerely,

Helen Kalkstein Fragiadakis

Directions

1. At the first class meeting, the students (and maybe also the teacher) should fill out the questionnaire below (or an adapted form).
2. At the second class, the students *Walk and Talk,* using the form on the next page. The items they ask are their responses taken from the questionnaires that they filled out at the first class meeting.

STUDENT QUESTIONNAIRE

What is your name?   (Last)_____   (First) _____

What name do you want everyone to call you in class? _____

Where are you from? _____

What is your native language? _____

How long have you been in this English-speaking country? _____

OR

Have you ever been in a country where English is the main language?

___Yes   ___No

If yes, where? _____

What language or languages do you speak at home? _____

Do you work? _____

If yes, what do you do? _____

Are you a high school or college student?   ___Yes   ___No

If yes, what are you studying? _____

What do you like to do in your free time?

What is something interesting about you or someone in your family?

What do you want to learn in this class?

Is there anything that you would like to add? If yes, please write it here.

Stand up, get out of your seat, and get to know your classmates. Find out the information in this Walk and Talk activity by talking to at least five different students. The questions you ask are based on the student questionnaires that you previously completed.

Steps

- Get up and ask a student the first question.
  If the student says "Yes," then ask "What's your (first) name?" If necessary, also ask "How do you spell that?" Then write the student's first name on the line at the right. If a student says "No," say "Thanks anyway" and move on to another student.
- Continue until you have a name next to each question.
- After everyone is finished, your teacher can ask for the names of students who said 'Yes' to each question and ask them for more information.

SAMPLE

Find someone who . . .   **First Name**

1. is from Mexico
   (Are you from Mexico?)   _____

2. speaks three languages
   (Do you speak three languages?)   _____

3. speaks a little bit of English at home
   (Do you speak a little bit of English at home?)   _____

4. is a cook/manicurist/doctor/businessman/businesswoman
   (Are you a doctor?)   _____

5. plays the guitar
   (Do you play the guitar?)   _____

6. has four sisters and five brothers
   (Do you have four sisters and five brothers?)   _____

7. speaks Japanese
   (Do you speak Japanese?)   _____

8. plans to get a degree in engineering
   (Do you plan to get a degree in engineering?)   _____

What's Wrong?

Theme:
Starting a New Class

Warm-Up

Answer these questions with a partner or in a small group.

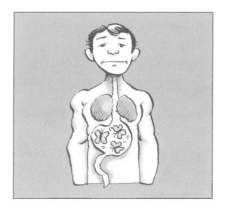

1. If this is your first day or first week of school,

    a. are you excited?   Yes   A little   No

    b. are you worried about homework and tests?   Yes   A little   No

    c. do you feel nervous?   Yes   A little   No
        (=do you have butterflies in your stomach?)

2. In your native country, do students stand up when the teacher enters
   the room? If yes, do you think it's a good idea?

3. In your native country, is it possible for students to call their teachers
   by their first name? What name does the teacher of *this* class want
   you to use?

Before You Listen

Look a the cartoon on page 1. It is the first day of school. Andrea and Eric are talking to each other. What do you think they are saying?

As You Listen

I,I

(A) Close your book. Listen to the conversation between Andrea and Eric to find the answers to these questions.

What is Eric worried about?   How does Andrea help him?

(B) Listen again, but this time read the conversation as you listen.

ANDREA:	**What's wrong,** Eric?
ERIC:	I'm really nervous. I'm always this way on the first day of school.
ANDREA:	You're not the only one. It's hard for me, too. I'm glad we're **taking** this **class** together.
ERIC:	Do you know anything about the teacher?
ANDREA:	Uh-huh, a little. Someone told me she gives a lot of homework, and you **have to** talk a lot in class.
ERIC:	Oh, no! **I'm afraid of** talk**ing** in front of a lot of people.
ANDREA:	Oh, **don't worry.** Everyone's afraid **at the beginning**, but after you **get to know** the people and **make friends** . . .
ERIC:	It doesn't **get better** for me. I'm shy. I **have trouble** look**ing** at people when I talk, and my hands shake.
ANDREA:	Look . . . the teacher's here. Let's talk after class.

Uh-huh = yes
Uh-uh = no

After You Listen

(A) Read the sentences about the conversation. Circle *T* for *true,* *F* for *false,* or *?* if you don't know.

1. Eric is worried and shy, and Andrea is helping him.   T   F   ?
2. Andrea is not nervous.   T   F   ?
3. Eric will make many friends in this class.   T   F   ?

4. The teacher wants students to talk in this class.   T   F   ?
5. Eric and Andrea are best friends.   T   F   ?

(B) Say the conversation in pairs. Then have two students say the conversation in front of the class.

Understanding the New Expressions

Work with Others

If you're working with a partner or in a small group, read the short dialogues and examples for each expression aloud. Also, complete the Your Turn exercises together. Then, for each expression, circle *Yes* or *No* to show if you understand. If you circled *No,* highlight or underline what is unclear, and ask questions about what is not clear.

Figure It out on Your Own

Read the short dialogues and examples for each expression. Also complete the Your Turn exercises that don't need partners. Then, for each expression, circle *Yes* or *No* to show if you understand. If you circled *No,* highlight or underline what is still unclear, and ask questions in class about what is not clear.

1. **Whát's wróng? = Whát's the mátter?**—Ask this question when you see a person with a problem.

    A: **What's wrong?**
    B: I have a headache.
       I feel sick.
       My test was hard.
       I'm tired.
       My car doesn't work.
       I'm angry with my sister.

    Similar Expression: **Whát's wróng with = Whát's the mátter with (someone or something)?**

    A: **What's wrong with** your son? He looks unhappy.
    B: He is. He doesn't want to go to the doctor today.

    A: **What's wrong with** the computer?
    B: I don't know. I dropped it and now it doesn't work.

ALL CLEAR ?

Yes   No

Your Turn

Think about your friends and family. When do you say, "What's wrong?"

I ask "What's wrong?" when *someone is crying.*
someone looks sad.
someone is _____.
someone looks _____.

2. **táke (a/this/that) cláss/táke clásses**—when you are in a class you *take* it. **(past = took)**

- I'**m taking this class** because it's very interesting.
- I **took that class** last semester.
- I'**m taking:**
  –only one **class** because I have a job.
  –three **classes,** so I have a lot of homework.

Your Turn

Answer in full sentences.

- How many classes are you taking right now?

_____

- What class(es) are you taking?

_____

- Did you take any classes last year?
  (If *yes*, add how many classes you took last year.)
  (If *no*, say *why* you didn't take any classes last year.)

_____

3. háve to/don't have to—Say "have to" to show that something is necessary. **(past = had to/didn't have to)**

Grammar Notes: After the infinitive *to,* always use the simple form of the verb. For example, it is correct to say, "In school, a student **has to go** to classes." It is not correct to say, "has to goes," and it is not correct to say "had to went." Look at the two lists below:

In school, you	*a student (he/she)*
have to	**has to**
had to	**had to**
go to classes	go to classes
study	study
do homework	do homework
talk in class	talk in class
take tests	take tests

Pronunciation: You *don't have* to say this, but many native speakers say:
I/you/we/they "have to" = "hafta"
she/he/it "has to" = "hasta"

Your Turn

What are things that teachers and students *have to* and *don't have to* do?

Students have to

_____

A teacher has to

_____

Students don't have to

_____

A teacher doesn't have to

_____

4. be afráid of (+ noun)—Use this expression when you are frightened by something. **(past = was or were)**

CONTRACTIONS WITH *BE*		
Affirmative	**Negative (Present)**	**Negative (Past)**
I am/I'm	I'm not	I wasn't
he is/he's	he's not/he isn't	he wasn't
she is/she's	she's not/she isn't	she wasn't
it is/it's	it's not/it isn't	it wasn't
we are/we're	we're not/we aren't	we weren't
you are/you're	you're not/you aren't	you weren't
they are/they're	they're not/they aren't	they weren't

Grammar Note: Use a noun or gerund (verb + ING) after *afraid of:*

be afraid of + noun	**be afraid of + verb + ING**
I'm afraid of earthquakes.	I'm not afraid of flying.
He isn't afraid of you.	He's afraid of walking alone at night.
We're afraid of tests.	We aren't afraid of taking the test.
She wasn't afraid of the big dog, but she is afraid of it now.	She was afraid of getting married, but she isn't afraid now.
They were afraid of snakes when they were young.	They weren't afraid of talking to the teacher, but they are now.

Your Turn

In the left column, write what you are and are not afraid of. Then get into a group with two classmates. In the other columns, write what they are and are not afraid of.

You	**Classmate 1**	**Classmate 2**
I'm afraid of _____. (noun)	_____ is afraid of _____. (noun)	_____ is afraid of _____. (noun)
I'm not afraid of _____. (noun)	_____ isn't afraid of _____. (noun)	_____ isn't afraid of _____. (noun)
I'm afraid of _____. (verb + ING)	_____ is afraid of _____. (verb + ING)	_____ is afraid of _____. (verb + ING)
I'm not afraid of _____. (verb + ING)	_____ isn't afraid of _____. (verb + ING)	_____ isn't afraid of _____. (verb + ING)

Write sentences about you and your two classmates. Start your sentences with some of the following:

We are all afraid of _____ .

None of us are afraid of _____ .

_____ and I are (aren't) afraid of _____ .

They are both afraid of _____ .

They aren't afraid of _____ .

5. **Dón't wórry (about)**—Use this expression to help someone not be afraid of something.

ALL CLEAR ?
Yes   No

   A: I don't want to fly.
   B: **Don't worry!** Flying is safe.

   A: **Don't worry about** the test. You'll do a good job.
   B: I hope so.

   A: **Don't worry about** me. I know what to do.
   B: Good. I'm glad to hear that.

   Similar Expression: **be wórried about**

   A: **I'm worried about** my family. There's bad weather in my country right now.
   B: Can you call them?

   A: What's wrong with him?
   B: He**'s worried about** his classes. They are very hard.

Your Turn

What situations make you nervous? Finish these dialogues.

   A: _____

   B: Don't worry!

   A: What are you worried about?

   B: I'm _____ .

6. **at the begínning (of)**—Use this expression when you want to talk about what happened at the start of an event.

- I was at a party last Saturday. **At the beginning,** everyone was quiet. But after an hour, the party was noisy.
- **At the beginning of** the party, everyone was quiet.

Contrast the Opposite: = **at the énd (of)**

- The party was quiet at the beginning, but it was noisy **at the end.**
- **At the end of** the party, everyone was happy.

Your Turn

Ask a partner these questions. Write his or her answers in complete sentences.

- How do you feel at the beginning of summer?
- How do you feel at the end of summer?

7. **gét to knów (a person or people)** = start to know more and more about someone **(past = got)**

TEACHER: I want to **get to know** you, so I'm going to ask you a few questions, OK?
STUDENT: OK.
TEACHER: Where are you from? What do you do? Do you like living here?

A: How's your class?
B: It's great. **I'm getting to know** more students, so I'm happy.

Your Turn: Listening Challenge

Listen to the short conversation. Two people are asking questions because they want to **get to know** each other. Which question is first? Which question is second? As you hear each question, put a number on the line.

_____ Where are you from?   _____ And you?
_____ Why not?   _____ How about you?
_____ What's your name?   _____ When did you come to the United States?
_____ Do you like it here?

I,2

8. **máke friénds (with)**—First you meet a person, and then maybe you will make friends with him or her. To do this, you ask questions to get to know each other, and if you like each other, you "make friends." **(past = made)**

ALL CLEAR ?
Yes No

A: I'm not happy here. I don't know anyone.
B: You need to **make friends.** When you have some friends, you'll feel better.

A: It's hard to **make friends with** people here. People say they will call or visit, but they don't.
B: I know. But you can **make friends.** You just need time.

Your Turn: Walk and talk

Walk around the classroom and ask four different students the questions below. Ask each student one question. Take short notes about what they say. When you finish, share what students said with the class.

Questions	Notes
1. Does it take a long time for you to make friends, or do you make friends easily (with no trouble)? Why?	**Name:**
2. In what kinds of places can you make friends?	**Name:**
3. How can you make friends? What can you say?	**Name:**
4. When you were younger, did you make friends with people that your parents liked or didn't like? Give an example.	**Name:**

9. **gét bétter** = improve **(past = got)**

   • I had a bad cold, but I **got better** quickly.

   A: It's very hard for me to speak English.
   B: Don't worry. Your English will **get better** every day.

   A: I wasn't happy here when I first arrived, but my life **got better** and I'm happy now.
   B: That's good to hear.

Your Turn

Complete these sentences. Share your writing with a partner. Give your partner some details to explain what you are saying.

   • My life can get better if _____.
   (Use a subject + present tense verb.)

   • My life got (better) (worse) when _____
   (Use a subject + past tense verb.)

   because _____.
   (Use a subject + past tense verb.)

10. **háve tróuble (__ING)** = **háve próblems (__ING) (past = had)**
    I **have trouble** talk***ing*** in class.

    speak***ing*** English.

   Similar Expressions:

   • She **has problems** sleep***ing*** when it is noisy.
   • He **has a hard time** understand***ing*** people when they speak fast.

   Note: You can also say "have trouble *with* (something)" and "have trouble *when* __:"

   • I often **have trouble *with*** my homework.
   • She **has trouble *when*** she speaks English.

Your Turn

Complete the sentences about yourself. Then share your sentences with a partner. Write sentences about your partner.

You	Your Partner
1. I have trouble _____	_____
2. I have problems _____	_____
3. I have a hard time _____	_____

NEW EXPRESSION COLLECTION

What's wrong?	don't worry (about)	get better
What's the matter?	at the beginning	have trouble
take a class	at the end	have problems
have to	get to know	have a hard time
be afraid of	make friends	

Exercises   *(See page 157 for pronunciation exercises for Lesson 1.)*

1,3

1. Mini-Dialogues

   Read the sentences in Column A. Choose the *best* response from Column B. To check this exercise, say each mini-dialogue with a partner. One student will read a line from Column A, and another student will answer with a line from Column B.

1A	1B
___ 1. I'm afraid of talking on the phone in English.	a. That's great!
___ 2. It's hard to get to know people when you live in a big city.	b. I have trouble getting to know people, too.
___ 3. What's wrong?	c. Don't worry. You'll see them again.
___ 4. I'm sorry, but I can't come. I have a cold.	d. Don't be afraid. You can do it.
___ 5. At the beginning, I always said, "Sorry, I don't speak English."	e. I'm afraid of dogs. Can you take him away?
___ 6. I don't want to leave! I made a lot of friends here.	f. But now what do you say?
___ 7. He can come with us tonight. He doesn't have to work.	g. I hope you get better soon.

2. Grammar Practice

Follow the directions and complete the sentences.

Directions	Sentences
1. Use past tense.	a. I (take) _____ a lot of classes last year. b. She (have to) _____ take five classes. c. He (negative: have to) _____ take a lot of classes. d. They (have) _____ a hard time with Exercise 1. e. She (be) _____ afraid of her teacher. f. We (negative: be) _____ worried about our test. g. The baby (get) _____ better very fast. h. They (negative: get) _____ to know each other at work. i. The children (make) _____ friends at school.
2. Add a preposition.	a. I don't know what's wrong _____ my car. I have to go to the mechanic. b. Are you afraid _____ snakes? c. They're very worried _____ money. d. At the beginning _____ class, everyone was talking. e. They made friends _____ each other very quickly. f. Can you help me? I'm having trouble _____ this.
3. Add a gerund (verb + ING)	a. Are you afraid of (fly) _____? b. Do you have a hard time (study) _____? c. Does she have trouble (understand) _____ English? d. Sometimes I have a hard time (speak) _____ English.

3. Error Correction

Find the errors and make corrections. One item is correct.

class

1. He's taking an English ~~classes~~.

2. Last year I take a swimming class.

3. What wrong with her? She looks very unhappy.

4. He have to go home after school every day.

5. They had to went home early yesterday.

6. I'm not afraid speaking English.

7. Are you afraid of speak English?

8. We are worried for our next test.

9. At beginning of the story, everyone was happy.

10. At the end the story, everyone was sad.

11. Don't worry. You will meet many new friends at your school.

12. You don't have trouble speak English.

4. Listen and Write the Expressions

Now it's after class, and Andrea and Eric are having lunch in the cafeteria. They are talking about their first class.

As you listen, fill in the blanks with the expressions that you hear. Be sure to use a capital letter at the beginning of each sentence. When you finish, perform the conversation with a partner.

1,4

ERIC: (1) _____, Andrea?

ANDREA: Now (2) _____ our class. The teacher said we
                (3) _____ do a lot of homework.

ERIC: (4) _____! I can help you. I think the class
                will be good, and we're going to (5) _____
                there.

ANDREA: Eric, you're funny. (6) _____, you
                (7) _____, and now you're fine. What happened?

ERIC: I don't know. I enjoyed talking to the students, and I want to
                (8) _____ them. Maybe I won't
                (9) _____ talking in this class. I wasn't very
                nervous after the first five minutes.

ANDREA: That's great. I can see you're happy that you (10) _____
                this class. I think your English will (11) _____
                very quickly.

ERIC: I hope you're right.

5. Sentence Writing

Write sentences or mini-dialogues with expressions from this lesson.
Use the New Expression Collection list on page 11.

I,5

6. Dictation

You will hear the dictation three times. First, just listen. Second, as you listen, write the dictation on a piece of paper. Skip lines. Third, check what you wrote.

Key Words: Eric, nervous, afraid, friends

After the dictation

Proofread

• Did you indent the first line of each paragraph?
• Does every sentence start with a capital letter?
• Do the names have capital letters?
• Does each sentence end with a period?

Check what you wrote.

• Circle your mistakes. Don't erase them.
• Look at your mistakes. What do you have to be more careful about next time?

_____ spelling   _____ vocabulary

_____ plurals   _____ verb tenses

_____ subject-verb agreement   _____ punctuation

_____ Other: _____

7. Walk and Talk

1. Use the following dialogue to get to know at least four of your classmates. Walk around the room and complete the conversation with different students.

   A: Hi, I'm _____. What's your name?
   B: I'm _____. It's nice to meet you.
   A: Nice to meet you, too. Where are you from?
   B: I'm from _____. How about you?
   A: I come from _____. Do you have trouble speaking English?
   B: Sometimes. That's why I'm taking this class.
   A: It's the same for me. Well, it was nice talking to you. See you later.
   B: See you.

2. Write sentences about the four students you talked to in Number 1. For example:

   a. Mario is from . . .

   b. Chen comes from . . .

   c. Sachiyo sometimes has trouble . . .

   d. Kate is taking this class because . . .

8. Group Survey

1. Work in groups of three or four. Write the first names of the group members on the top lines of the chart. Choose one student to be the leader. The leader will interview one person at a time. Each student in the group will listen and write short notes under each person's name.

Culture Note

When you are listening, make eye contact, nod, and smile. In the United States, eye contact shows that you are interested.

Notes are . . .

(1) short—not full sentences.

(2) just a few words so you can remember information later.

Questions	Student Name	Student Name	Student Name	Student Name
1. Why are you taking this class?				
2. Is there anything about this class that you are afraid of? If yes, what? Why?				
3. What do you have to do so your listening and speaking will get better?				
4. What do you have the most trouble with in English? Why?				

2. Choose one student to be the reporter. The reporter tells the class some of your group's answers. The reporter should look at the class and not read. It is not necessary to say students' names when giving this report.

Culture Note

When you are speaking, make eye contact with your listeners.

Examples:

Students in my group are taking this class because . . .

One person in my group is afraid of . . .

Two people in my group are going to . . . so their listening and speaking will get better.

We have trouble with . . .

9. Write a Dialogue

Write a conversation on your own or with a partner. Give the people names, and use at least five of the expressions from the box.

Start with *"What's wrong?"*

have to	be afraid of	don't worry
at the beginning	at the end	get to know
make friends	have trouble	be worried about
get better		

10. Word Search

Complete the underlined expressions. Then find the complete expressions in the puzzle. The words can be spelled backwards. They can also be vertical (↕), horizontal (↔), or diagonal (↗) (↖).

I. You look upset. <u>**What's**</u> _____?

2. <u>**At the**</u> _____ of the party, I was quiet.

3. <u>**At the**</u> _____ of the party, I was tired because I danced a lot.

4. They _____ **trouble** understanding TV programs.

5. She said you have a cold. I hope you _____ **better** soon.

6/7. It's hard to _____ **friends**, but we <u>**have**</u> _____ try.

8. He wants to _____ **a class** so he can learn to cook.

9. I want to _____ **to know** everyone in my class.

10. _____ **about** your English!

II. Are you _____ **about** school?

```
N  I  P  M  H  G  D  J  H  S  R  M  J  B  Y
Y  H  V  C  A  E  L  E  A  D  D  B  T  E  D
Z  W  F  Q  B  T  Q  J  V  N  Y  D  U  G  S
J  W  B  H  H  B  I  F  E  E  G  O  O  N  V
K  Z  V  A  J  E  C  X  T  I  G  N  B  O  U
X  K  L  V  Q  T  V  O  R  R  E  T  A  R  T
D  N  E  E  H  T  T  A  O  F  T  W  D  W  A
T  I  Y  T  H  E  U  W  U  E  T  O  E  S  K
Z  Q  Z  O  V  R  P  O  B  K  O  R  I  T  E
J  G  J  F  T  K  O  W  L  A  K  R  R  A  A
C  N  L  V  E  M  T  I  E  M  N  Y  R  H  C
V  L  M  B  P  U  R  R  P  Y  O  I  O  W  L
J  B  F  T  G  G  D  A  R  C  W  L  W  Y  A
A  T  T  H  E  B  E  G  I  N  N  I  N  G  S
Y  G  R  R  B  E  A  F  R  A  I  D  O  F  S
```

11. Make a Speech—Appendix C

Prepare a five minute speech about one of the following topics. (See Appendix C on page 177 for more information.) Talk about one of these things:

- A class that I once took
- A time that I was afraid (or nervous)
- Classroom customs in my native country

12. Hot Seat—Appendix D

Interview a classmate. Choose one student to come to the "Hot Seat" (a chair) in the front of the room. Or, get into groups and choose one student in each group to be on the "Hot Seat." This student will answer questions. See Appendix D on page 182 for sample questions. It is best to *not* ask personal questions.

Who's This?

Theme: Making
Telephone Invitations

Warm-Up

Answer these questions with a partner or in a small group.

- How do you feel when you speak English on the phone?
- What is more difficult for you—having a conversation on the phone in English, or leaving someone a recorded message in English? Why?

Circle what you think are the correct answers.

I.   When you want to ask who is calling you, you can say:

(a) Who are you?   (b) Who's this?

2.   When you say your name on the phone, you can say:

(a) I am __.   (b) This is __.

3.   When you ask someone on the phone to wait, you can say:

(a) Wait please.   (b) Just a minute.

Focused Listening

Before You Listen

Look at the right side of the cartoon above. Alex and Sara are talking on the phone. What do you think they are saying?

As You Listen

(A) Close your book. Listen to the conversation between Anna and Alex and then Alex and Sara to find the answers to these questions.

Why is Alex calling?   Does Sara want to see Alex?

(B) Listen again, but this time read the conversation as you listen.

ANNA: (SARA'S SISTER)	Hello.
ALEX:	Hi, Sara.
ANNA:	**Who's this?**
ALEX:	**It's** Alex.
ANNA:	Oh, hi, Alex. **This is** Anna. **Hold on** a minute and I'll get Sara . . . Sara, **it's for you!** . . .
SARA:	**I'll be right there** . . . . Alex? Hi!
ALEX:	Hi, Sara. Want to go to the movies Friday night?
SARA:	I'm really sorry, but I **can't make it** Friday night . . . How about Saturday?
ALEX:	Sure. **Why don't I pick you up** at 7:00?
SARA:	**That sounds** great. Oh, Alex, I'm sorry. My parents are calling me for dinner and I have to **get off.** See you Saturday.
ALEX:	Great. See you. Bye.

After You Listen

(A) Answer these questions with short *yes* or *no* answers. Use *is, are, does,* or *can* (and their negative forms if necessary). Check your answers with a partner.

1. Is Alex calling Sara? _____ Yes, he is. _____

2. Is Anna Sara's sister? _____

3. Does Alex want to go to the movies with Sara? _____

4. Does Alex want to go to the movies with Anna? _____

5. Can Sara go to the movies on Friday night? _____

6. Can she go to the movies on Saturday night? _____

7. Is Alex going to drive? _____

8. Is Sara going to drive? _____

9. Are Sara and Anna going to have dinner soon? _____

(B) Say the conversation with two other students. Then have three students say the conversation in front of the class.

Understanding the New Expressions

Work with Others

If you're working with a partner or in a small group, read the short dialogues and examples for each expression aloud. Also, complete the Your Turn exercises together. Then, for each expression, circle *Yes* or *No* to show if you understand. If you circled *No*, highlight or underline what is unclear, and ask questions about what is not clear.

Figure It out on Your Own

Read the short dialogues and examples for each expression. Also complete the Your Turn exercises that don't need partners. Then, for each expression, circle *Yes* or *No* to show if you understand. If you circled *No*, highlight or underline what is still unclear, and ask questions in class about what is not clear.

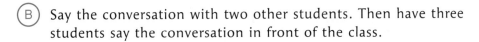

1. **Whó's thís? = Who is this?**—You can ask this when you don't know who is calling on the phone.

   Note: When you don't know who is *at the door*, you ask, "Who's there?" or "Who is it?"

   A: Hi. Can (*Or:* May) I please speak to Daniel? (*Or:* Can/May I speak to Daniel, please?)
   B: **Who's this?**
   A: It's Melissa.

   Similar Expressions: **Whó's cálling? Can I ásk whó's cálling? May I ásk whó's cálling?**

   These expressions are formal. They are usually used by businesses and people who don't know each other.

More Formal

- Hello.
- Who's calling?
- Mr. Brown

Informal

Hi.
Who's this?
Jim

Your Turn

What are the best questions to ask in these telephone conversations?

A: Computers Incorporated.
B: Hello. May I please speak to Ms. Williams?
A: _____?
B: This is her son.
A: One moment, please.

A: Hello.
B: Hi. Can I speak to Steve, please?
A: _____?
B: It's his sister.
A: Sure. Just a sec. (Just a second.)

ALL CLEAR ?

Yes   No

2. **It's __; This is __.** You say these expressions after someone asks you, "Who's this?"

Note: It is *not* correct to say "I am" when you give your name on the phone.

A: Hello.
B: Hello. May I speak to Alex Nicholas, please?
A: **This is** Alex. (*OR:* This is he. *OR:* Speaking.)
B: This is Bill from Computers Incorporated. I'm calling to tell you that your computer is ready.

A: Hello.
B: Hi. May I please speak to Sara?
A: Who's this?
B: **It's** Alex. (*OR:* **This is** Alex.)
A: Just a moment. (*OR:* I'm sorry. Sara can't come to the phone right now. Can I take a message?)

Culture Note

It is more polite to say someone "can't come to the phone right now" than to say someone is "busy."

Your Turn

Have a phone conversation with a partner. Use one of the dialogues above as a model. Your partner will answer the phone, and you will ask to speak to a famous person. Your partner will ask who you are.

A: Hello.
B: _____
A: _____
B: _____
A: _____

3. **hold ón**—Say this when a person calls and you want that person to wait a minute. **(past = held)**

Note: It is not correct to say "Wait."

A: Hello.
B: Hello. This is Melissa. May I speak to Daniel, please?
A: Sure. **Hold on** and I'll get him.

Sometimes when you are on the phone with a business, you will hear this:

• Doctor's Office. Can you hold?
• Please hold, and someone will be with you shortly (soon).

Related Telephone Expressions:
• **ánswer the phóne** or **ánswer it**
• **gét the phóne** or **gét it** = answer the phone or answer it
• **hang úp** = finish your call and put the receiver (the part that you hold next to your ear) back on the phone **(past = hung)**

— Daniel, the phone's ringing. Can you **answer (get) it?**
— Alex, when are you going to **hang up?** I need to use the phone!

> *Pronunciation:* When you say *answer,* don't pronounce the 'w.'

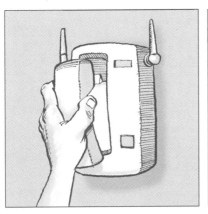

Note: You can also "hang up" clothes in a closet on a clothes hanger.

Your Turn

Finish these three dialogues with "hold on," "answer the phone," and "hang up."

A: Wait! Don't _____! I want to talk to him.
B: OK. Don't worry. He wants to talk to you, too.

A: Anna. Can you _____? My hands are wet.
B: Sure. Hello . . .

A: Hi, can I please speak to Jon?
B: Sure. _____.

4. **It's for (yóu)!** = The phone call is for you.

A: Hurry up! **It's for you!**
B: I'm coming.

A: Who is it? **Is it** for me?
B: No, **it's for me.**

Similar Expressions: to announce that a phone call is for someone

- Sara! **There's a call for you!**
- Alex! **Phone's for you!**
- Anna! **Telephone!**

Your Turn

Get into groups of three. Give each student a number: 1, 2, or 3. Use your real names. Complete the conversation.

Speaker (Ring)	Conversation
(Student 1) _____ (name)	Hello.
(Student 2) _____ (name)	Hi. This is _____. (name of Student 2)
	Can I please speak to _____? (name of Student 3)
(Student 1) _____ (name)	Sure. Just a minute.
	_____, (name of Student 3) _____!

5. **I'll be ríght thére.** = I'm cóming.

Note: You cannot change this sentence. It is not correct to say, "I'll be right there in five minutes." When you say, "I'll be right there," you are saying that you will be there immediately.

A: Hurry! The phone's for you.
B: **I'll be right there.**

Your Turn

Say these lines with a partner.

A	B
1. It's time to go.	I'll be right there.
2. We're leaving.	I'll be right there.
3. Everyone is ready for dinner.	I'll be right there.
4. Can you help me with my homework?	I'll be right there.
5. _____.	I'll be right there.

6. **can/cán't máke it** = can/can't go somewhere **(past = could/couldn't)**

A: **I can make it** on Monday, but not on Tuesday.
B: Monday's fine.

A: There's a great concert on Saturday night.
B: On Saturday night? Oh I'm sorry. **I can't make it.** I already have plans.
A: That's too bad.

Your Turn

Complete this conversation with a partner. Follow the example above.

A: There's a _____ on _____.
B: On _____? Oh, I'm sorry. _____.
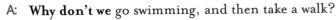
_____.
(give a reason)
A: That's too bad. Maybe next time.

7. **Why dón't . . . ?**—This is a way to give ideas about things to do. These ideas are called "suggestions."

A: **Why don't we** go swimming, and then take a walk?
B: Great idea!

A: **Why don't you** go to the bank, and I'll go to the post office?
B: I don't know. Let's go together.

1,7

Your Turn: Listening Challenge

Read the list of suggestions below. Then listen to six sentences. After you hear each sentence, give a suggestion from the list. Write the letter of the suggestion next to the number of the sentence that you hear.

	Sentence Number	Suggestions
C	1	a. Why don't you go to bed?
_____	2	b. Why don't you get something to eat?
_____	3	c. Why don't we go to the beach?
_____	4	d. Why don't you take lessons?
_____	5	e. Why don't they go to the movies?
_____	6	f. Why don't we study together?

ALL CLEAR ?

8. **pick (someone) úp** = get someone, often by car

A: I'll **pick you up** in front of the cafe at 4 o'clock, OK?
B: Thanks a lot. That will be a big help.

• She **picked up** her brother.
• She **picked her brother up** at school.
• She **picked him up.**

Don't say, "She picked up him." Pronouns have to go in the middle.

pick	**me**	up
	you	
	him	
	her	
	it	
	them	
	us	

Your Turn

Put a check (√) next to the correct sentences. Put an X next to the incorrect sentences. Make corrections.

Sentences   **Corrections**

_√_ 1. I'll pick you up later.

_X_ 2. I'll pick up you tomorrow.   I'll pick you up tomorrow.

_____ 3. She pick her children up
          every day after school.

_____ 4. She picks up them every
          day after school.

_____ 5. My friend pick him up yesterday.

_____ 6. Can you pick me up at 5:00?

9. **Thát sóunds** _____! = In my opinion that is _____.
   (adjective) (adjective)

   A: I can pick you up at 10:00, and then we can go to the beach.
   B: **That sounds great!**

   A: I was in traffic for three hours.
   B: **That sounds terrible!**

   A: The movie was about life in a college dorm.
   B: **That sounds interesting.**

ALL CLEAR ?
Yes   No

Your Turn

Respond with "That sounds great/terrible/interesting."

                                                      That sounds . . .

• It rained for two weeks when I was on vacation.   _____

• After lunch, we went to the park and then we went
  to a movie.   _____

• I met a lot of people from many different countries. _____

• _____.   _____

10. **get óff (the phone) = hang úp** (See Number 3.) **(past = got)**
    • I'm sorry, but I have to **get off** the phone. It's already midnight.
    • After she **got off** the phone, she went shopping.

    Note: You can also **get off** a bike, a horse, a bus, a train, and an airplane,
    but you "get out of" a car.

ALL CLEAR ?
Yes   No

Your Turn

Is there anyone in your family who often doesn't want to get off the phone? If yes, who? What do you say to him or her when you want to use the phone?

NEW EXPRESSION COLLECTION

Who's this?	hold on	It's for you!
Who's calling?	answer the phone	I'll be right there.
It's . . .	get the phone	That sounds great!
This is . . .	hang up	get off the phone
pick up	Why don't . . .?	can/can't make it

Exercises

(See page 159 for pronunciation exercises for Lesson 2.)

1,8

1. Mini-Dialogues

    Read the sentences in Column A. Choose the *best* response from Column B. To check this exercise, say each mini-dialogue with a partner. One student will read a line from Column A, and another student will answer with a line from Column B.

1A	1B
___ **1.** Can you come on Sunday?	**a.** I'll be right there.
___ **2.** Bill, it's for you!	**b.** OK. I'll talk to you tomorrow. Bye.
___ **3.** Why don't I pick you up after school?	**c.** Who's this?
___ **4.** Sorry. I have to get off because I need to pick Jim up.	**d.** Sure. I'll get it.
	e. I'm sorry, but I can't make it.
___ **5.** Hello. Can I please speak to Ann?	**f.** Thank you. That's really nice of you.
___ **6.** Can you answer the phone?	

2. Grammar Practice

Follow the directions and complete the sentences.

Directions	Sentences
1. Use past tense.	a. The secretary told me to hold on. Well, I (hold) _____ on for ten minutes, and then I (hang) _____ up. b. He had to work late, so he (can't) _____ make it to the party. c. When she (get) _____ off the phone, she watched TV for a while.
2. Add a preposition.	a. When she called, I asked her to hold _____, but she hung up! b. Jan! Telephone! It's _____ you! c. Can you get _____ the phone? I need to talk to you.
3. Add contractions: *don't, there's, I'll, Who's, can't, it's*	a. Don't leave without me. _____ be right there! b. Why _____ we study together? c. We _____ make it tonight, but how about tomorrow? d. Suzanne, _____ a call for you. e. Suzanne, _____ for you! f. _____ this?

3. Error Correction

Find the errors and make corrections. Every item has *one* mistake.

     I'll
1. ~~I~~ be right there.
2. A: Hello.   B: Hi. Can I please speak to Katie?   A: Who are you?
3. A: Hello.   B: Hi. Is Katie there?   B: Yes, wait a minute.
4. Hello. I am Steve. Can I speak to Mike?
5. Wait! Don't hang the phone! I want to speak to Mom, too!
6. My hands are wet. Can you open the phone?
7. I'm sorry. I can't make on Monday, but I can be there on Tuesday.
8. Why we don't have coffee after class?
9. They picked up me in front of my house.
10. A: I'm late because I was in traffic for two hours.

    B: That sound terrible!
11. Sorry. I need to get of the phone because it's time for dinner.
12. Julie — This telephone call is for you!

4. Listen and Write the Expressions

Alex and Sara had dinner together on Saturday. Now it's Sunday and they are talking on the phone.

As you listen, fill in the blanks with the expressions that you hear. Be sure to use a capital letter at the beginning of a sentence. When you finish, perform the conversation with two classmates.

SARA'S SISTER: Hello.

ALEX: Hi. Can I speak to Sara, please?

SARA'S SISTER: (1) _____?

ALEX: (2) _____ Alex.

SARA'S SISTER: (3) _____ a second . . . Sara!

(4) _____! It's Alex.

SARA: (5) _____ . . . Hi, Alex.

ALEX: Hi, Sara. How are you doing?

SARA: Fine. How about you?

ALEX: Pretty good. I had a really great time last night.

SARA: I did too. That's a great restaurant.

ALEX: I know. (6) _____
we go back there next weekend?

SARA:	(7) _____
	great. When?
ALEX:	Is Friday OK? I can (8) _____
	at 7:00 again.
SARA:	Why don't *I* drive this time? I'll pick *you* up at 7:00.
ALEX:	That's fine with me. I'll be waiting for you. Take care . . .
SARA:	Alex? Wait . . . Don't (9) _____.
	There's one more thing. Last week, *you* paid for dinner.
	This time, *I* want to pay.
ALEX:	Sara! No!
SARA:	Yes! Listen, . . .

Culture Question

In your native country, can a woman be the driver when there is a man in the car? When a man and woman are out to dinner, can the woman pay?

5. Sentence Writing

Write sentences or mini-dialogues with expressions from this lesson. Use the New Expression Collection list on page 28.

6. Dictation

You will hear the dictation three times. First, just listen. Second, as you listen, write the dictation on a piece of paper. Skip lines. Third, check what you wrote.

I,10

Key Words: answers, Saturday, restaurant

Punctuation words:
period .
comma ,
open quote "
closed quote "
question mark ?
exclamation point !

After the dictation

Proofread
- Did you indent the first line of each paragraph?
- Does every sentence start with a capital letter?
- Do the names have capital letters?
- Does each sentence end with a period?

Check what you wrote
- Circle your mistakes. Don't erase them.
- Look at your mistakes. What do you have to be more careful about next time?

____ spelling   ____ vocabulary
____ plurals   ____ verb tenses
____ subject-verb agreement ____ punctuation
Other: _____

7. Walk and Talk

1. Ask two students from the other side of your classroom the questions below. Take short notes in the chart.

Ask: **What's your first name? How do you spell it?**

	Classmate 1	Classmate 2
About Phones 1. What kinds of phones do you and your family have? 2. What kinds of things can your phone do? 3. What kind of phone do you think is the best? Why?		
About Invitations In Exercise 4, Sara told Alex that she wanted to drive and that she wanted to pay for dinner. 4. Do you think it's OK for a woman to be the driver when she is in a car with a man? Why or why not? (And how do you feel about female pilots?) 5. Do you think it's OK for a woman to ask a man for a date? Why or why not? 6. Do you think it's OK for a woman to pay when she is on a date? Why or why not?		

2. Write six sentences about what one of the students said to you in Number 1 above. For example:

_____'s phone can _____.

_____ thinks it's OK for a woman to ask a man for a date because _____.

8. Role Play: Giving an Invitation

Directions:

1. Get into groups of four. Two students will be Listeners, and the other two students will be Phone Partners A and B. The Phone Partners will put their chairs back-to-back, just as you see in the cartoon. On their desks, they should have the list of Lesson 2 expressions from page 28.

2. *Phone Partner A:* Call Phone Partner B. Ask how he or she is and then invite him or her to do something this weekend.

   Phone Partner B: Tell A that you can't make it on Saturday, but that you can make it on Sunday. Talk about the details of your plans.

   Listeners: Keep a paper and pen on your desk. Write down expressions from this lesson as you hear the Phone Partners use them.

3. *Listeners:* After the Phone Partners finish their conversation, share the list of the new expressions that you heard. Comment on the conversation.

4. Reverse roles. Listeners become Phone Partners and repeat steps 1 to 3.

Places to go:
to the city
out to dinner
to the movies

Things to do:
go dancing
go shopping
study together

Starting lines	Ending lines
R i n g . . . A: Hello. B: Hi. This is . . . . Can I please speak to . . .?	A: Well, thanks for calling. B: My pleasure. See you . . . .

9. Write a Dialogue

The girl on the couch has just answered the phone. The call is for her brother. The person calling invites her brother to go out and do something, but he doesn't want to or can't go. You decide. Write a conversation on your own or with a partner. Give the people names, and use at least five of the expressions from the box.

Start with *"Hello."* (Also, try to use some expressions from Lesson 1.)

| Who's this? | This is ____ | hold on | It's for you! |
| pick up | That sounds ____. | get off | can't make it |

10. Unscramble and Find the Secret Message

Unscramble the words and write them in the puzzle. Then find the secret message at the bottom of the page.

LOHD NO

GANH PU

HOW'S GCLLAIN

CPIK PU

EGT FFO

HOW'S SITH

THSI SI

TI'S FOR OYU!

I'LL BE HGRTI HEETR.

CAN'T MEKA IT

SRWANE HET HEOPN

WHY NOD'T

11. Make a Speech—Appendix C

Prepare a five minute speech about one of the following topics. (See Appendix C on page 177 for more information.) Talk about one of these things:

- An electronic item that I own (e.g., phone, computer, MP3 player). (Talk about how it works, what it can do, or how it changed your life.)
- Male and female roles at home and at work in my native country.

12. Hot Seat—Appendix D

Interview a classmate. Choose one student to come to the "Hot Seat" (a chair) in the front of the room. Or, get into groups and choose one student in each group to be on the "Hot Seat." This student will answer questions. See Appendix D on page 182 for sample questions. It is best to *not* ask personal questions.

Collocation Match-Up

Collocations are special combinations of words. Collocations can be idioms or other phrases and expressions. Find collocations from *Lessons 1* and *2* by matching the words in Column A with words in Column B. Sometimes more than one answer is possible. (You will probably be able to make additional expressions that are not from Lessons 1 and 2. Put these in the box.)

A

1. get _____better_____
2. get _____
3. get to _____
4. worry _____
5. That sounds _____
6. at the _____
7. at the _____
8. What's _____
9. I'll be _____
10. take an _____
11. Who's _____
12. Who's _____
13. be afraid _____
14. hold _____
15. have _____
16. have _____
17. pick _____
18. It's _____
19. can't _____
20. make _____
21. hang _____

B

wrong?

English class

great!

of

about

beginning

end

to do something

know someone

friends

better √

trouble speaking

this?

calling?

up

up

on

right there.

for you.

off the phone

make it

Additional Collocations

Crossword Puzzle

Across

2 Can you hold ___ a minute?

3 Last year we ___ to know many people at our school.

5 Sorry, I need to get ___ the phone and do my homework.

7 We can't ___ it tomorrow. We're sorry.

10 I'll be right ___.

12 Who's ___?

13 Why ___ I pick you up in front of the theater?

15 Everyone is ___ of earthquakes.

18 This ___ Janet.

21 At the ___, English was hard.

22 We ___ to drive five hours yesterday.

Down

1 Don't worry ___ this class.

2 I'm not afraid ___ dogs.

4 At ___ end of the movie, everyone was crying.

6 When are you going to ___ off the phone? I need it!

8 Can you ___ the phone?

9 I have trouble ___ these expressions.

11 That ___ wonderful.

14 I'm sorry you're sick. I hope you get ___ soon.

16 She made a lot of ___ in her class.

17 She's ___ three classes.

19 I'll be ___ there.

20 I'm almost at the ___ of the book.

Let's Go Away for the Weekend!

Theme: Making Plans for the Weekend

Warm-Up

Answer these questions with a partner or in a small group.

What do you like to do when you have free time? Look at the 12 activities below. Next to each, write a number (1, 2, or 3) to show if you don't like it, if it's just OK, or if you like it a lot.

1	2	3
I don't like it.	It's just OK.	I like it a lot.

_____ 1. go to the movies	_____ 5. go swimming	_____ 9. take walks
_____ 2. go to the beach	_____ 6. go shopping	_____ 10. play soccer
_____ 3. go to the park	_____ 7. go jogging	_____ 11. read a book
_____ 4. go to the mall	_____ 8. go hiking	_____ 12. clean my room

When you finish, tell members of your group what you like to do and what you don't like to do. For example, you can say:

When I have free time, I like to _____.

I don't like to _____.

Before You Listen

Look at the cartoon on page 39. Peter and Alice are talking about going away for a weekend. What do you think they are saying?

As You Listen

I, II

(A) Close your book. Listen to the conversation between Peter and Alice to find the answers to these questions.

Where are they going to go next month?
What season (fall, winter, spring, or summer) is it now?

(B) Listen again, but this time read the conversation as you listen.

PETER:	You know, we have a three-day weekend next month. Do you want to **go away**?
ALICE:	That's a great idea! Where do you want to go?
PETER:	To the beach.
ALICE:	The beach in the winter?
PETER:	We don't have to **go swimming**. We can **take walks** on the beach.
ALICE:	But **what else** can we do?
PETER:	Oh, there are **plenty** of things to do. We can read, go to the movies. I need to relax, don't you?
ALICE:	I sure do. You're right. The beach is a good idea. And it won't **be crowded**. Do you think we need to **make a reservation** anywhere?
PETER:	No, I don't think so. There are **lots of** places to stay. And they'll be cheaper now than they are in the summer.

After You Listen

(A) Below are details about the introductory conversation. Circle *T* for *true, F* for *false,* or *?* if you don't know.

1. Peter and Alice will go away for a week.   T   F   ?

2. Alice is surprised because Peter wants to go
   to the beach in the winter.   T   F   ?

3. Alice doesn't want to go to the beach in the winter.   T   F   ?

4. Peter and Alice go away often.   T   F   ?

5. There will be many people at the beach.   T   F   ?

(B) Say the conversation in pairs. Then have two students say the conversation in front of the class.

Understanding the New Expressions

Work with Others

If you're working with a partner or in a small group, read the short dialogues and examples for each expression aloud. Also, complete the Your Turn exercises together. Then, for each expression, circle *Yes* or *No* to show if you understand. If you circled *No,* highlight or underline what is unclear, and ask questions about what is not clear.

Figure It out on Your Own

Read the short dialogues and examples for each expression. Also complete the Your Turn exercises that don't need partners. Then, for each expression, circle *Yes* or *No* to show if you understand. If you circled *No,* highlight or underline what is still unclear, and ask questions in class about what is not clear.

1. **gó awáy (for)**—Use this expression to describe when you leave home and sleep in a different place for one or more nights. **(past = went)**

ALL CLEAR ?

Pronunciation: When you say *went away,* connect the two words so they sound like one word: went‿away.

A: What's the suitcase for?

B: I'**m going away** for a few days. My sister is getting married.

A: Have a great trip!

A: Ruth, we'**re going away** for the weekend. Can you take care of the dog?

B: Sure. No problem.

A: How was your weekend?

B: It was great. We **went away** for a few days.

Similar Expressions: **gó on a tríp** (to), **táke a tríp** (to), **gó** (to)

A: What are you going to do this weekend?

B: We're going to
$\left.\begin{array}{l} \textbf{go on a trip} \\ \textbf{take a trip} \\ \textbf{go} \end{array}\right\}$ to Disneyland.

A: Where did they go?

B: They
$\left.\begin{array}{l} \textbf{went on a trip} \\ \textbf{took a trip} \\ \textbf{went} \end{array}\right\}$ to Disneyland.

Similar Expressions: **have a vacation, take a vacation, be on vacation**

- He looks relaxed because **had a long vacation.**
- I'm so tired. I need to **take a vacation.**
- Jennifer **is on vacation** for two weeks.

Culture Note

Many Americans who work have two weeks of vacation every year. How many weeks do working people in your native country usually have for vacation?

Your Turn

With a partner, answer these questions.

1. Do you ever have vacations, or do you always work?
   If you have vacations, how long are they?

2. Imagine that you have a two-week vacation. Do you want to go away or stay home? Why?

3. When you go away, do you usually:
   - stay with friends or relatives?
   - stay at a hotel or motel?
   - go camping?

   Why?

2. **gó** swímm**ing**—Use "go ___ing" to talk about *activities that you dó* (not places).

Grammar note: It is not correct to say "go *to* ___ing."

A: It's such a hot day! Do you want to **go swimming** after class?

B: That's a good idea. Do you want to go to the beach or to a pool?

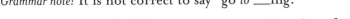

GO HIKING   GO ICE SKATING

Activity	**Place**
go shopping	go to a store; go to a mall
go jogging	go to a park
go fishing	go to a river
go swimming	go to a swimming pool or a beach
go hiking	go to the mountains
go ice skating	go to a skating rink
go dancing	go to a club

Your Turn

Fill in the blanks with *go* or *go to.*

1. _____ the mountains

2. _____ a club

3. _____ ice skating

4. _____ a river

5. _____ shopping

6. _____ dancing

7. _____ swimming

8. _____ a store

3. **táke wálks**—You take walks for pleasure or exercise. You can *take a walk* to the park, but you don't *take a walk* to work. You *walk* to work. **(past = took)**

A: What do you do to get exercise?

B: Well, I go swimming when I can, and I **take** (long) **walks.**

Grammar Notes:
- *Walk* in "take a walk" is a noun.
- Singular: *take a walk*
- Plural: *take walks*

Similar Expression: **gó for a wálk**

- It's a beautiful evening. Do you want to { **take a walk** / **go for** } around the block?

- We { **took** / **went for** } a long **walk** yesterday afternoon. It was great.

Your Turn

Write sentences with these expressions. Remember to use *took* or *went* if you are talking about the past.

1. take a walk

   _____

2. take walks

   _____

3. go for a walk

   _____

4. go for walks

   _____

4. whát élse = what more/what other things

   A: Let's see . . . we have bread, salad, and juice. **What else** do we need?
   B: Uh, I think we need some rice, but that's all.

   A: What did you do over the weekend?
   B: Well, let's see. I cleaned my house and did my laundry.
   A: **What else** did you do?
   B: Oh, yes! I almost forgot. I went to a great party.
   A: I'm glad you did something that was fun.

Your Turn

Complete the dialogue. Use the simple present tense because you are talking about a routine—what you do in *every* class.

   A: What do you do in your class?
   B: Oh, we talk a lot.
   A: _____ do you do?
   B: We _____ and _____.

5. plénty of = more than enough (more than you need)

   A: I think we need to buy more rice.
   B: No, we don't. Look—we have **plenty of** rice right here.
   A: Really? Oh, I didn't see it.

   A: Mom, I'm bored. I have nothing to do.
   B: Oh, there are **plenty of** things to do. You can clean your room, take out the garbage, and walk the dog. When you finish doing all that, tell me, and I'm sure I'll find more for you to do.

Your Turn

Complete this chart. Put checks (✓) on the lines that describe you. Then compare yourself to your partner.

1. Do you have enough	No, I don't have enough	Yes, I have enough (just right)	Yes, I have plenty of (more than enough)
• homework?	_____	_____	_____
• money?	_____	_____	_____
• free time?	_____	_____	_____
2. Did you have enough	**No, I didn't have enough**	**Yes, I had enough (just right)**	**Yes, I had plenty of (more than enough)**
• sleep last night?	_____	_____	_____
• breakfast this morning?	_____	_____	_____
• to do last weekend?	_____	_____	_____

ALL CLEAR ?

6. be crówded = be full of people

Contrast parts of speech: adjective—*crowded*
                             noun—*a crowd; crowds*

- This restaurant **is crowded.** Let's go somewhere else.
- In the winter, the beach **isn't crowded.**
- Let's go home. This party **is** too **crowded.**
- I'm tired. I had to stand on the bus all the way home because it **was** so **crowded.**

- There is a big **crowd** near that car. Maybe someone famous is in the car.
- I don't like **crowds,** so I want to stay home on New Year's Eve.

Your Turn

Ask three students the questions below. Complete the chart.

Classmates	What kinds of places can be crowded?	How do you feel when you are in a crowd?
1. _____	_____	_____
2. _____	_____	_____
3. _____	_____	_____

7. **máke a reservátion (for)** = save a place for someone **(past = made)**

ALL CLEAR ?

    A: Hello. Rivoli's.
    B: Hi. I'd like to **make a reservation** for Saturday night.
    A: Sure. What time?
    B: 7:30 for six people.
    A: And your name?
    B: Rose.
    A: OK. That will be six people for 7:30 on Saturday night. See you then.
    B: Thanks a lot.

    A: Hello. Seaside Hotel.
    B: Hi, I'd like to **make a reservation** for two people on July first.
    A: Could you please hold on a minute? I'll connect you with reservations.

Your Turn

Use the conversation on the previous page as an example to make a reservation at a restaurant.

A: Hello. _____.

B: Hi. I'd like to make a reservation for _____.

A: Sure. _____?

B: _____.

A: And your name?

B: _____.

A: OK. That will be _____ on _____.
See you then.

B: Thanks a lot.

Your Turn: Listening Challenge

I,12

Someone is on the phone making a reservation at a restaurant. First, read the four questions. Then listen. After you listen, answer the questions.

1. Why is the caller making a reservation? _____

2. Who will go to the restaurant with the caller? _____

3. Where does the caller want to sit in the restaurant? _____

4. What time and day is the reservation for? _____

ALL CLEAR ?

Yes   No

Pronunciation: Lots of is often pronounced "lotsa" or "lotsuv." When you write, write "a lot of."

8. lóts of = a lót of = many/much

A: We had **lots of** (a lot of) homework last night, didn't we?
B: Uh-huh. I worked on it for two hours!

A: How was your weekend?
B: Oh, we had **lots of** (a lot of) fun. We went hiking and swimming. It was great. Do you want to come with us the next time we go?

Your Turn

What do you like?

_____ 1. lots of parties   _____ 4. lots of traffic

_____ 2. lots of tests   _____ 5. lots of free time

_____ 3. lots of books to read   _____ 6. Other: _____

NEW EXPRESSION COLLECTION

go away	take walks	make a reservation
go on a trip	what else	lots of
go swimming	plenty of	a lot of
go for a walk	be crowded	take a trip

Exercises   *(See page 160 for pronunciation exercises for Lesson 3.)*

1. **Mini-Dialogues**

   Read the sentences in Column A. Choose the *best* response from
   Column B. To check this exercise, say each mini-dialogue with a partner.
   One student will read a line from Column A, and another student will
   answer with a line from Column B.

1,13

A	B
___ 1. We went shopping and then we went out to lunch.	a. She's on vacation until next Monday.
___ 2. Do we need to leave now?	b. No, we have plenty of time. We can leave in a half hour.
___ 3. That restaurant is always crowded. Do you think we need to make a reservation?	c. Not everywhere. I'm sure we can find a quiet place to go.
___ 4. I'm full. Does anyone want to take a walk with me?	d. What else did you do?
___ 5. Lots of people want to go away in the summer. That's why it's so crowded everywhere.	e. Great idea. I'll be right there.
	f. I know. But I don't have any more vacation days this year.
___ 6. You're working too hard. You need to take a vacation.	g. That's a good idea. I'll call right now.
___ 7. Where's Sherry?	

2. Grammar Practice

Follow the directions and complete the sentences.

Directions	Sentences
1. Use past tense.	a. Last year, they (go) _____ away for the whole summer. b. We (take) _____ a trip to the mountains for the weekend. c. I wasn't here for the meeting because I (be) _____ on vacation last week. d. I (negative: have) _____ my vacation in July. I (have) _____ it in August. e. We (go) _____ swimming in a river. We (negative: go) _____ swimming in a lake. f. The plane (negative: be) _____ crowded. g. I (make) _____ the reservation for 8:00.
2. Add a preposition.	a. Wow! You went away _____ a month? b. She went _____ a trip _____ South America. c. They're not home. They're _____ vacation. d. I need to go _____ a walk. I need exercise. e. Stay for dinner. Don't worry. We have plenty _____ food. f. Did you make a reservation _____ 7 o'clock or _____ seven people? g. His plane ticket cost a lot _____ money.
3. Add an article.	a. He went on _____ short trip to his native country. b. They took _____ expensive vacation. c. Let's take _____ long walk. d. I need to make _____ reservation. e. _____ lot of people travel in the summer.

3. Error Correction

Find the errors and make corrections. Every item has *one* mistake.

1. We went for a walks yesterday.

2. It's a beautiful day. Let's go for walk.

3. They took a walked yesterday.

4. They go to shopping every Saturday morning.

5. Our teacher gives us plenty homework.

6. The party very crowded. Let's go home.

7. There are a lot people at the party.

8. There is lots good food at the party.

9. There are plenty drinks at the party.

10. I called the restaurant and make a reservation for four people.

11. The store is closed. They are in vacation for two weeks.

12. They go on trip to San Francisco every year.

4. Listen and Write the Expressions

Peter from the introductory conversation is now talking to his friend Bonnie at work. It is Monday, and he is telling her about the great weekend that he had with his wife, Alice.

As you listen, fill in the blanks with the expressions that you hear. When you finish, perform the conversation with a partner.

PETER: Hi, Bonnie. How was your weekend?

BONNIE: Pretty good. I stayed home and relaxed. How about you? Did you and Alice (1) _____?

PETER: Uh-huh. We found a small town near the beach and stayed in a nice motel for three nights. It was great, and it wasn't expensive.

BONNIE: What did you do at the beach? Wasn't it cold?

PETER: Yeah, a little. We didn't (2) _____. But we (3) _____. And we got (4) _____ fresh air.

BONNIE: That sounds great. At this time of year, it probably (5) _____ _____.

PETER: No, it wasn't.

BONNIE: So, (6) _____ did you do?

PETER: Well, let's see . . . on Saturday night, we (7) _____ at a club, and on Sunday we (8) _____. It was a lot of fun.

BONNIE: It sounds like you had a great weekend. Can you give me the name of the motel? Maybe Ed and I can go there sometime.

5. Sentence Writing

Write sentences or mini-dialogues with expressions from this lesson. Use the New Expression Collection list on page 49.

6. Dictation

1,15

You will hear the dictation three times. First, just listen. Second, as you listen, write the dictation on a piece of paper. Skip lines. Third, check what you wrote. *Key Words:* weekend, ice skating

After the dictation, proofread. Circle your mistakes. Don't erase them. Think about what you need to study.

7. Walk and Talk

1a. Imagine that it is Friday. First, complete this dialogue. Then, get up and walk around the room. Say (don't write) the dialogue with at least three different students. Your dialogues will all be different. Take turns being Speaker A or Speaker B. If you don't understand what someone says, say "Could you please repeat that?"

A: What are you going to do this weekend?
B: I'm going to _____.
A: What else are you going to do?
B: I'm going to _____. How about you?
A: I'm going to _____ and _____.
B: That sounds _____ (great/interesting). Have a good time!
A: You too. Nice talking to you. See you.
B: It was nice talking to you, too. Have a good weekend.

1b. Complete the chart about things your classmates are going to do this weekend.

Name	Fun/Enjoyable activity	Necessary activity
Julia is going to	go shopping	clean

1c. Imagine that it is Monday. Complete this conversation. Say (don't write) the dialogue with at least three different students. Your dialogues will be different. Remember to use the past tense.

A: How was your weekend?

B: It was _____. (great, pretty good, OK, terrible)

A: What did you do?

B: I _____.

A: What else did you do?

B: I _____.

A: Did you have a good time?

B: _____. (Yes, it was fun/interesting. OR: No, not really.) How about you? What did you do?

A: I _____.

B: That sounds _____. Well, it was nice talking to you. See you.

A: See you.

1d. Complete the chart about things your classmates did last weekend.

Name	Fun/Enjoyable activity	Necessary activity
Julia	went shopping	cleaned

2. Write what your classmates said to you in Part 1. Use the students' names.

First, write sentences about what three students are going to do this weekend.

* _____
* _____
* _____

Second, write sentences about what three students did last weekend.

* _____
* _____
* _____

8. Info Gap—
   How was your summer?

Imagine that the summer is over and now you are back at school. You see a friend and talk about your summer.

One of you will be Speaker 1 and the other will be Speaker 2. Speaker 1 will look at page 173 and Speaker 2 will look at page 174. You will have different information to give each other. Don't look at your partner's page.

When you finish, find a new partner and tell that person about your first partner's summer.

9. Write a Dialogue

Work on your own or with a partner. Write a conversation between Bonnie from Exercise 4 and her husband Ed. Bonnie is suggesting that they go away because they work too much and are very tired. Use at least five of the expressions from the box.

Start with "Why don't we . . ." (Also, try to use some expressions from other lessons that you studied.)

go away	go on a trip	take a trip	take a vacation	take walks
What else?	plenty of	be crowded	make a reservation	lots of

10. Tic-Tac-Toe

a. Your teacher will put tic-tac-toe lines on the board, with expressions in the nine spaces.

b. The class should be divided into two teams, *X* and *O*. Flip a coin (choose "heads or tails") to see which team goes first.

c. To get an *X* or an *O* in a space, a team has to make a sentence with the expression in that space. The sentence should be correct in grammar and meaning. Team members can plan what they will say for up to 30 seconds. Students should take turns giving the answers.

d. The first team to get three *X*'s or *O*'s in a straight line wins. The line can be horizontal (↔), vertical (↑), or diagonal (↗) (↖).

e. When you finish a game, if there are any expressions that are not covered by *X*'s or *O*'s, you can keep them for another game. You can add other expressions to the spaces already used and play again.

go away for	take a trip to	went shopping
took a walk	on vacation	plenty of
be crowded	make a reservation	lots of

11. Make a Speech—Appendix C

Prepare a five minute speech about one of the following topics. (See Appendix C on page 177 for more information.) Talk about one of these things:

- A trip that I once took
- My first impressions of a country
- A place in my native country that I recommend for tourists
- How to pack a suitcase

12. Hot Seat—Appendix D

Interview a classmate. Choose one student to come to the "Hot Seat" (a chair) in the front of the room. Or, get into groups and choose one student in each group to be on the "Hot Seat." This student will answer questions. See Appendix D on page 182 for sample questions. It is best to *not* ask personal questions.

Lesson 4

Wake Up!

———————

Theme: Describing Your Daily Routine

Warm-Up

Answer these questions with a partner or in a small group.

1. Do you have trouble getting up in the morning? Why or why not?

2. In the morning, what do you do first? What do you do second?

Number the following. Put the numbers on the lines at the left. Everyone will have different answers.

__1__ a. wake up

_____ b. wash your face

_____ c. get up

_____ d. brush your teeth

_____ e. take a shower

_____ f. go to school or go to work

_____ g. get dressed (put on clothes)

_____ h. eat breakfast

_____ i. shave (Of course, not everyone does this.)

Before You Listen

Look at the cartoon on page 57. Mike and Tom are talking. What do you think they are saying?

As You Listen

1,16

(A) Close your book. Listen to the conversation between Mike and Tom to find the answers to these questions.

Why does Tom need to get up?   Why is Tom having trouble getting up?

(B) Listen again, but this time, read the conversation as you listen.

> MIKE: **Wake up,** Tom! Don't you have to go to the airport?
>
> TOM: Yeah, I'll **get up** in five minutes. I don't want to **get out of bed**—it's so early.
>
> MIKE: Well, I'**m going back to sleep.** I hope you won't miss your plane. **Have a good trip.**
>
> TOM: Thanks.
>
> (Tom's thoughts—Oh, why did I **go to bed** so late last night? It's so hard to **get up,** and it's so cold and dark. But I need to get up now and **take a shower.** What time is it . . . ? 6 o'clock? Oh, no! I'm late. I **don't have time for** a shower. I have to **get dressed** and get to the airport right away.)

After You Listen

(A) Below are details about the introductory conversation. Circle *T* for *true, F* for *false,* or *?* if you don't know.

1.	Mike woke Tom up.	T	F	?
2.	Tom doesn't want to take a trip.	T	F	?
3.	Tom takes a shower before he goes to the airport.	T	F	?
4.	Tom went to bed late last night because Mike made a going-away party for him.	T	F	?
5.	Mike can go back to sleep, but Tom can't.	T	F	?

(B) Say the conversation in pairs. Then have two students say the conversation in front of the class.

Work with Others

If you're working with a partner or in a small group, read the short dialogues and examples for each expression aloud. Also, complete the Your Turn exercises together. Then, for each expression, circle *Yes* or *No* to show if you understand. If you circled *No*, highlight or underline what is unclear, and ask questions about what is not clear.

Figure It out on Your Own

Read the short dialogues and examples for each expression. Also complete the Your Turn exercises that don't need partners. Then, for each expression, circle *Yes* or *No* to show if you understand. If you circled *No*, highlight or underline what is still unclear, and ask questions in class about what is not clear.

1. **wake úp** = open your eyes after sleeping **(past = woke up)**

ALL CLEAR ?

A: What time do you **wake up** every day?
B: At about 7:00. How about you?

A: I like weekends because I can **wake up** late.
B: What time do you usually **wake up**?
A: About 11:00.

Pronunciation: Stress the second part of this phrasal verb: wake UP. (See page 159.)

A: I didn't sleep well last night.

B: Why not?

A: I **woke up** a lot because my roommate was snoring.

wake someone úp = wake another person

Grammar Note: Remember that pronouns go *between* the parts of verbs with two parts.

wake	**me**	up
	you	
	him	
	her	
	it	
	us	
	them	

A: Shh! The baby's sleeping. Don't **wake her up!**

B: Sorry. I didn't know.

A: I'm going to take a nap. Can you **wake me up** in an hour?

B: Sure.

Opposite: **fáll asléep (past = fell)**

- Children often **fall asleep** when they are riding in cars.
- The movie was very boring, so I **fell asleep.**
- I went to bed at 11:00, but I **fell asleep** around 1:00 because I was thinking a lot about my life.

Related Expressions: **stay úp** = not go to sleep (not go to bed)

sléep láte = sleep ín (get up late in the morning)

- They **stayed up** late last night, so they are tired today.
    (= They went to bed late.)
- She's tired, so she wants to **sleep late (sleep in)** tomorrow morning.
    (= She wants to get up late tomorrow morning.)

Contrast: **sleep late** = get up late (maybe 11:00 A.M.)

go to sleep late = go to bed late (maybe 2:00 A.M.)

Your Turn

Ask your partner these questions. Write the answers on the right.

Questions	Answers
1. What time did you wake up this morning?	I woke up at _____.
2. Did a person wake you up?	Yes No
3. Did an alarm clock wake you up?	Yes No
4. What time did you fall asleep last night?	I fell asleep at around _____.
5. Do you often stay up late on weekends? (If yes, why?)	Yes No _____
6. Do you ever sleep late (sleep in) on Sundays? (If yes, how late?)(=until what time?)	Yes No _____

2. **get úp** = get out of bed after you wake up **(past = got up)**

A: **Get up,** Sandy! You'll be late for school!

B: I am up Mom.

A: I'm going to bed early tonight because I have to **get up** early tomorrow.

B: Why?

A: I have an appointment.

A: What time did you wake up this morning?

B: Well, I woke up at 6:00, but I **got up** at 7:00.

A: Why?

B: I wasn't in a hurry so I listened to the radio.

A: You look sleepy.

B: I am. I **got up** at 5:00 this morning.

A: Really? Why?

B: I started an exercise program.

Opposite: **gó to béd** (See number 6.)

ALL CLEAR ?

Your Turn

Ask your partner these questions. Write the answers on the right.

Questions	Answers
1. What time did you get up this morning?	I got up at _____.
2. What time do you usually get up on weekdays?	I usually get up at _____
3. What time do you usually get up on weekends?	I usually get up at _____

ALL CLEAR ?

3. get óut of béd = leave one's bed

Note: It is not correct to say get out of ~~the~~ bed.

• It's so cold in here! I don't want to **get out of bed.**

A: Every night three-year-old Jamie **gets out of bed** and goes into his parents' bed.
B: Is that OK with his parents?

Your Turn

Ask three classmates:
When is it hard for you to get out of bed? Why?

ALL CLEAR ?

4. gó báck to sléep = go to sleep again after you wake up **(past = went)**

A: Dad, wake up! I had a bad dream.
B: Relax. It was just a dream. Now, **go back to sleep.** Everything is OK.

A: Why are you watching TV at 3 o'clock in the morning?
B: I woke up and can't **go back to sleep.**
A: Do you want some tea?
B: Oh, that sounds nice. Thanks.

Your Turn

Ask a partner: When you wake up in the middle of the night, is it usually hard for you to go back to sleep? If it is hard, what can you do to get sleepy?

5. Háve a góod (great) tríp! = You say this when someone is going to leave and travel somewhere.

ALL CLEAR ?
Yes No

A: Do you have your ticket?
B: Yes.
A: Do you have enough money?
B: Uh-huh.
A: Do you have your toothbrush?
B: Listen, I have to go now.
A: Bye. **Have a good trip!** Call me when you get there.

Similar Expression: **táke a tríp** (See Lesson 3)

A: What are you going to do this weekend?
B: We're going to **take a trip** to the mountains.

Your Turn

Ask a partner: Imagine that someone just gave you $1,000. You want to use the money to take a trip. Where do you want to go?

Answer: I want to go to _____.
            I want to take a trip to _____.

6. gó to béd/gó to sléep = to get into bed and try to sleep **(past = went)**

ALL CLEAR ?
Yes No

Note: It is not correct to say go to ~~the~~ bed.

• When I take a nap in the afternoon, I can't **go to bed** early.

A: I'm tired. I'm **going to bed** (I'm **going to sleep.**)
B: But it's only 9 o'clock!
A: I know, but last night I **went to bed** very late.

Your Turn

Ask a partner these questions. Write the answers on the right.

Questions	Answers
1. What time did you go to bed last night?	I went to bed at _____ last night.
2. What time do you usually go to bed on weeknights?	I usually go to bed at _____ on weeknights.
3. What time do you usually go to bed on weekends?	I usually go to bed at _____ on weekends.

ALL CLEAR ?

7. **néed to** = necessary—You "need to" do something when it is necessary.

A: I **need to** go to the airport.
B: What time? I can take you.
A: Really? Thanks!

Grammar Note: Put the base form of the verb after *to*. Don't add *-s*, *-ing*, or a past form:

She needs to go.
She needs to ~~goes~~.
She needs to ~~going~~.
She needed to ~~went~~.

He **needs to** { sleep.
be on time.
learn English.

If you don't use *to*, then put a noun after the word *need*.

He **needs** { money.
a car.
time to learn English.

Your Turn

Answer these two questions.

1. What are three things that you need to do today?
   I need to _____, _____,
   and _____.

2. What are three things that you need when you go on a trip?
   I need _____, _____,
   and _____ when I go on a trip.

8. táke a shówer—Use this expression when you want to get in the shower to get clean. **(past = took)**

TAKE A SHOWER

TAKE A BATH

Similar Expression: **táke a báth**

A: What do you do after you get up?

B: I wash my face, brush my teeth, and **take a shower.** Sometimes I **take a bath.**

Your Turn

Ask your partner these questions.

1. What do you like better—to take a shower or to take a bath? Why?

2. How long are you usually in a shower? in a bath?

3. Do you sing in the shower?

9. háve tíme for (something)/háve tíme to (do something) = not be busy

A: Do you **have time** for a cup of coffee?

B: Sure. Great idea!

A: Sorry, I **don't have time** to eat breakfast. I'm late.

B: Here, take some toast with you.

A: Thanks. See you.

Grammar Note: After *have time for,* add a noun.
                    After *have time to,* add the base form of the verb.

Have time FOR something	**Have time TO DO something**
Do you have time for *a cup of coffee?*	Do you have time *to drink* a cup of coffee?
I don't have time for *breakfast.*	I don't have time *to eat* breakfast.

Your Turn

Are you a very busy person? On the left, write three things that you don't have time for, and on the right, write three things that you don't have time to do. Then compare yourself to your partner.

I don't have time for (noun)   **I don't have time to (verb)**

_____   _____

_____   _____

_____   _____

ALL CLEAR ?

Yes   No

10. gét dréssed = put on your clothes

A: Let's go!

B: Wait! I have to **get dressed** first. I'm still in my pajamas.

Contrast: **put ón** (specific clothes) **(past = put)**

Note: When you say "get dressed," you mean that a person puts on all of his or her clothes. When you say "put on," you mean that a person puts on specific clothes, such as socks:

> She is getting dressed. (general)
> She is putting on her socks. (specific clothes)

- He's only three years old, and he's learning to **get dressed.**
- He's only three years old, and he's learning to **put on** { his socks.
  { his shoes.

Note: When you "get dressed" or "put something on," you are using an action with your hands to put clothes on your body. After you "get dressed" or "put something on," you are *wearing* something. When you "wear" clothes, they are already on you. There is no action.

Opposite: **gét undréssed = take óff** (your clothes)

- He's only three years old, and he's learning to **get undressed.**
- He's only three years old, and he's learning to **take off** { his socks.
                                                                  his shoes.

Grammar Note: Remember that pronouns go *between* the parts of verbs with two parts:

Yes	Yes	Yes	No
put on your shoes	put your shoes on	put them on	put on them
put on your shirt	put your shirt on	put it on	put on it
take off your shoes	take your shoes off	take them off	take off them
take off your shirt	take your shirt off	take it off	take off it

Your Turn A

Next to each sentence, write *C* if the sentence is correct. Write *NC* if the sentence is not correct.

__C__ 1. He put on his shoes.

____ 2. He put on his jacket.

____ 3. He put his jacket on.

____ 4. He put it on.

____ 5. He put on it.

____ 6. The child took off his shirt.

____ 7. The child took it off.

____ 8. The child took off it.

____ 9. The child took his shirt off.

____ 10. The child got dressed.

Your Turn B: Listening Challenge

This is a dictation. Write the imperative sentences (commands) you hear. End each with an exclamation point (!).

1. _____
2. _____
3. _____
4. _____
5. _____

NEW EXPRESSION COLLECTION

wake (someone) up	go back to sleep	take a shower
fall asleep	have a good trip	have time for
stay up	take a trip	have time to
sleep late	go to bed	get dressed
get up	go to sleep	put on
get out of bed	need to	take off

Exercises

(See page 162 for pronunciation exercises for Lesson 4.)

1. Mini-Dialogues

Read the sentences in Column A. Choose the *best* response from Column B. To check this exercise, say each mini-dialogue with a partner. One student will read a line from Column A, and another student will answer with a line from Column B.

A	B
___ 1. Wake up! You're late!	a. Isn't that sweet! She fell asleep.
___ 2. What time did you go to bed last night?	b. Because I stayed up really late last night.
___ 3. Sorry, I don't have time to talk. I have to go to the airport.	c. Can you wait five minutes? I need to get dressed.
___ 4. Hurry up! Let's go.	d. I don't care. It's too cold to get up.
___ 5. It's really cold in here.	e. I really need to sleep late tomorrow. Can we go around noon?
___ 6. It's really hot in here.	f. Why don't you take off your sweater?
___ 7. Look at the baby.	g. Very late.
___ 8. Why are you so tired today?	h. Why don't you put on a sweater?
___ 9. Let's go shopping early tomorrow morning.	i. Have a great trip!

2. Grammar Practice

Follow the directions and complete the sentences.

Directions	Sentences
I. Use past tense.	a. She (go) _____ to sleep at 8:00 P.M. and she (wake) _____ up at 8:00 A.M. b. He worked all night and then he (fall) _____ asleep in class! c. I feel great because I (sleep) _____ really late today. d. I (get) _____ up at 5:00 because the phone rang. e. We (take) _____ off our shoes before we went into the house. f. She (put) _____ on two sweaters, but she was still cold.
2. Add a preposition.	a. It's late. I need to go _____ bed. b. When he got out _____ bed, he fell down. c. I'm late. I don't have time _____ breakfast. d. Put _____ a jacket! It's cold outside. e. Please take your shoes _____ before you come in.
3. Add a noun or pronoun. (More than one answer is possible.)	a. His alarm clock woke _____ up. b. Here are your shoes. Put _____ on. c. Put your _____ on. d. Take off your _____. e. Take your _____ off.
4. Add a noun or the base form of a verb. (More than one answer is possible.)	a. Do you have time to _____ me with my homework? b. Do you have time for _____? c. We need _____ if we want to take a big trip. d. We need to _____ our tickets soon.

3. Error Correction

Find the errors and make corrections. Every item has *one* mistake.

1. Mike wake up after Tom went to the airport.

2. Mike took shower and got dressed before he had breakfast.

3. He put warm clothes because it's cold today.

4. Every day he goes to work at 12:00. So he always has time read the newspaper in the morning.

5. When he gets home from work, he take off his work clothes and puts on blue jeans.

6. A: Does he wear blue jeans?

   B: Yes, he puts on them after he gets home from work.

7. Last night, he go to sleep late, so he's tired today.

8. Last night, he felt asleep at 3:00 A.M.!

9. He needs to sleeping more.

10. He always goes to the bed late.

11. When he sleeps later, he's late for work.

12. He's very busy. His girlfriend says he has no time to her.

4. Listen and Write the Expressions

Tom is now back from his trip. He went to his cousin's wedding. (His cousin got married.) Now he is talking to his roommate, Mike.

As you listen, fill in the blanks with the expressions that you hear. When you finish, perform the conversation with a partner.

MIKE: So, how was your trip?

TOM: Great. My cousin's wedding was really nice, and I saw a lot of my friends and relatives.

MIKE: Did you miss your plane?

TOM: You know, I almost did. I was really late because I didn't want to

(1) _____. Remember?

MIKE: Yeah. It was really cold and dark in here.

TOM: But I (2) _____ on the plane. When I

(3) _____,

I felt better. And when I got to my parent's house, it was great. We

(4) _____ to talk and relax.

I (5) _____ some of my old clothes and worked

in the garden. Then I (6) _____ and

(7) _____ for the wedding.

MIKE: What did you wear? Do you have any nice clothes?

TOM: Sure, I do. I have a suit, you know.

MIKE: I don't believe it. You (8) _____ show me some pictures
of you in a suit. I know you only in blue jeans.

5. Sentence Writing

Write sentences or mini-dialogues with expressions from this lesson.
Use the New Expression Collection list on page 68.

6. Dictation

You will hear the dictation three times. First, just listen. Second, as
you listen, write the dictation on a piece of paper. Skip lines. Third,
check what you wrote.

Key Words: airport, roommate, dark, lucky

After the dictation, proofread. Circle your mistakes. Don't erase them.
Think about what you need to study.

7. Walk and Talk

1. Ask five of your classmates the questions in the chart. Take very short notes in the spaces. Write the students' names on the right. After you collect the information, complete Number 2.

Grammar Reminders:

- Use simple present tense because you are talking about a habit or routine, something that you repeat (every day, every weekend). For example, "I usually *get up* at 7:30 on weekdays."
- Use the preposition *at* when you give a time (AT 7 o'clock) and use the preposition *on* when you give a day (ON weekdays, ON Sundays).

Questions	First Names
1. What time do you usually get up on weekdays?	_____
2. What time do you usually get up on weekends?	_____
3. What time do you usually go to bed on weekdays?	_____
4. What time do you usually go to bed on weekends?	_____
5. How many hours of sleep do you need every night?	_____
6. How many hours of sleep do you usually get every night?	_____
7. Do you often feel tired?	_____
8. If you said 'yes' to question 7, then what can you do to feel better?	_____

2. Complete these sentences about the students you talked to in Number 1. Give times or numbers in 1, 3, 5, 7, 9, 10, and 11. Give students' names in 2, 4, 6, and 8.

1. Most of the students get up between _____ and _____ on weekdays.

2. _____ gets up the earliest, and _____ gets up the latest on weekdays.

3. Most of the students get up between _____ and _____ on weekends.

4. _____ gets up the latest on weekends.

5. Most of the students go to bed between _____ and _____ on weeknights.

6. _____ goes to bed the earliest, and _____ goes to bed the latest on weeknights.

7. Most of the students go to bed between _____ and _____ on weekends.

8. _____ goes to bed the latest on weekends.

9. Most of the students need between _____ and _____ hours of sleep every night.

10. Most of the students get about _____ hours of sleep every night.

11. _____ out of five students often feel tired.

12. Students can feel better if they _____.

As a class:

- Compare your sentences.
- Answer this question: Do most students in your class usually get enough sleep?

8. Contact Assignment

With a partner, ask three native English speakers the following questions. You can ask people in your school, at a library or store, or in your neighborhood. You don't need to walk up to strangers on the street.

Introduce yourself like this. You can practice saying this in class:

Hi. We're from _____ and _____ and we're studying English. We have a homework assignment to ask eight short questions about what time people usually get up and go to bed. Do you have a minute to answer our questions?

Advice: Look directly at the people you are talking to and take short notes. Don't just look at your book, and don't let the people read the questions.

1. What time do you usually get up on weekdays?
2. What time do you usually get up on weekends?
3. What time do you usually go to bed on weekdays?
4. What time do you usually go to bed on weekends?
5. How many hours of sleep do you need every night?
6. How many hours of sleep do you usually get every night?
7. Do you often feel tired?
8. (If 'yes' is the answer to number 7) What can you do to feel better?

After you get the information from the three people, answer these questions.

1. Do the people you talked to usually get enough sleep? ____ Yes ____ No
2. If they don't get enough sleep, what do they need to do?
3. When you said you were studying English and you asked people to talk to you, what did they say?
4. Did the native English speakers understand your questions?

   ____ always   ____ usually   ____ sometimes   ____ rarely
5. How much did you understand when the native speakers answered your questions? ____ percent
6. How did you feel when you talked to the three native speakers?
7. If you do this kind of activity again, would you do anything differently? What?

9. Write a Dialogue

Work on your own or with a partner. Write a conversation between the mother and her son, Sam. Sam is sleeping late and his mother wants him to get up. Use at least five of the expressions from the box.

Start with *"It's 11:30 Sam!"* (Also, try to use some expressions from other lessons that you studied.)

get up	get dressed
fall asleep	stay up late
get out of bed	have time to/for
need (to)	sleep late
go back to sleep	wake up

10. Unscramble and Find the Secret Message

Unscramble the words and write them in the puzzle. *All of the verbs are in the past tense.* Then find the secret message at the bottom of the page.

TKOO A ERHSWO ▢▢▢▢ ▢ ▢▢▢▢▢▢
  26 29 28 38 39 50 3

TOKO A RTPI ▢▢▢▢ ▢▢▢▢
  35 16 48

OKOT FFO ▢▢▢▢ ▢▢▢
  18

NWTE TO PESLE ▢▢▢▢ ▢▢▢ ▢▢▢▢▢
  17

TWNE CKAB OT LSEPE ▢▢▢▢ ▢▢▢▢ ▢▢ ▢▢▢▢▢
  45 31 4

ELFL SLEAPE ▢▢▢▢ ▢▢▢▢▢▢
  15

LTESP AELT ▢▢▢▢▢ ▢▢▢▢
  36 42 11

EYDTSA PU ▢▢▢▢▢▢ ▢▢
  22 2 5 40

TGO TOU OF DEB ▢▢▢ ▢▢▢ ▢▢ ▢▢▢
  8

TGO PU ▢▢▢ ▢▢
  19 6

GTO RSDESDE ▢▢▢ ▢▢▢▢▢▢▢
  20 9 49

DNEEED OT ▢▢▢▢▢ ▢▢
  32 23 27 46 34 7

ADH EIMT TO ▢▢▢ ▢▢▢▢ ▢▢
  33 25 13 37 21 24 1 43

HDA IETM RFO ▢▢▢ ▢▢▢▢ ▢▢▢
  44 41 10 30

UPT NO ▢▢▢ ▢▢
  12

OWEK UP ▢▢▢▢ ▢▢
  47 14

▢▢▢▢▢ ▢▢ ▢▢▢ ▢▢▢ ▢▢▢▢ Y ▢▢ ▢▢▢▢
1 2 3 4 5 6 7 8 9 10 11 12 13 14 15 16 17 18 19 20 21 22 23

▢▢▢▢▢ ▢ ▢▢▢ ▢▢▢▢▢▢ Y , ▢▢▢▢▢▢ Y , A ▢▢
24 25 26 27 28 29 30 31 32 33 34 35 36 37 38 39 40 41 42 43 44 45 46

▢▢▢▢ .
47 48 49 50

11. Make a Speech—Appendix C

Prepare a five minute speech about one of the following topics. (See Appendix C on page 177 for more information.) Talk about one of these things:

- A typical weekday
- A typical Saturday or Sunday

12. Hot Seat—Appendix D

Interview a classmate. Choose one student to come to the "Hot Seat" (a chair) in the front of the room. Or, get into groups and choose one student in each group to be on the "Hot Seat." This student will answer questions. See Appendix D on page 182 for sample questions. It is best to *not* ask personal questions.

Collocation Match-Up

Collocations are special combinations of words. Collocations can be idioms or other phrases and expressions. Find collocations from *Lessons 3* and *4* by matching the words in Column A with words from Column B. Sometimes more than one answer is possible. (You will probably be able to make additional expressions that are not from Lessons 3 and 4. Put these in the box.)

A

1. take _____
2. take _____
3. take _____
4. take _____
5. take _____
6. take _____
7. go _____
8. go _____
9. go _____
10. go _____
11. make _____
12. get _____
13. get _____
14. get _____
15. have _____
16. Have _____
17. put _____
18. fall _____
19. wake _____
20. a lot _____
21. What _____
22. plenty _____
23. be _____
24. be _____

B

on your coat

off your sweater

of

of

a trip

on vacation

on a trip

a good trip!

a shower

a bath

dressed

a walk

else?

crowded

a reservation

away

up

up

out of bed

asleep

back to sleep

to bed

time for

a vacation

Additional Collocations

Crossword Puzzle

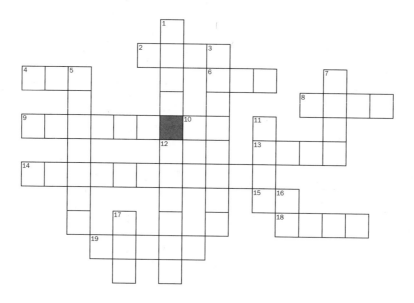

Across

2 The party was fun. There were ___ of people there.

4 It's time to go to ___.

6 Look! He's sleeping. Wake ___ up!

8 See you. I'm going ___ to sleep.

9 Stay for dinner. We have ___ of food.

10 I stayed ___ until 3:00 last night!

13 What ___ do you want to do?

14 I'd like to make a ___ for ten for dinner.

15 We need ___ study a lot.

18 The baby ___ asleep on the plane.

19 We're ___ on a trip for a few days. Can you watch the dog?

Down

1 We ___ a long walk and now we feel a lot better.

3 Do you want to go ___ on Saturday?

5 She got ___ really fast because she woke up late.

7 Do you want to ___ a trip with us?

11 We ___ away for two weeks and had a great time.

12 She's not here. She's ___ a two week vacation.

16 Sometimes it's hard to get out ___ bed.

17 I'm tired. I ___ up at 6:00.

Warm-Up

1. Answer these questions with a partner or in a small group.

    1. Do you like to eat in restaurants?

    2. How often do you eat out?

    3. What is your favorite restaurant?

    4. When you eat in a restaurant with a friend, do you usually:

        ___ a. pay the exact amount for your own meal?

        ___ b. "split the check" in half?

        ___ c. try to "treat" your friend (offer to pay for 100 percent)?

    5. The typical amount of a tip in the United States is 15 percent. Do you leave tips in your native country? If yes, how much is typical?

2. These are things that people say in a restaurant. Write *W* next to what a waiter or waitress will say. Write *C* next to what a customer will say.

___ 1. I'll be right with you.

___ 2. Can I get you anything to drink?

___ 3. We have some specials tonight.

___ 4. Are you ready to order?

___ 5. What is the soup of the day?

___ 6. What kind of salad dressing do you have?

___ 7. How would you like your hamburger?

___ 8. Would you like anything else?

___ 9. Can we have some more water please?

___ 10. Can we have the check please?

Before You Listen

Look at the cartoon on page 81. A brother and sister are talking at a restaurant. What do you think they are saying?

As You Listen

1,21

(A) Close your book. Listen to the conversation between the brother and sister to find the answers to these questions.

What are they celebrating?   Who's going to pay for lunch?

(B) Listen again, but this time, read the conversation as you listen.

SISTER:	Oh, it's so nice to **eat out** and have time together. What a great birthday present!
BROTHER:	I'm glad you like it. I'm always happy to **treat you to** lunch. And I was thinking, you know, we never really have time to just sit and talk.
SISTER:	I know. And now we have two hours! And this is a really nice place.
BROTHER:	Yeah, I come here **once in a while.**
SISTER:	So, what are you going to have?
BROTHER:	Um. . . I'm not sure yet. But you order **whatever you want.** It's your birthday.
SISTER:	Whatever I want? OK. But please don't sing Happy Birthday when we have dessert. If you do, I'll go under the table.
BROTHER:	You'll never change. Always so shy.
SISTER:	Well, that's me. Anyway, I think **I'll have** the chicken Caesar salad. What are you going to have?
BROTHER:	The salad sounds good. But I'm going to have soup too because I'm really **hungry.**

WAITRESS: Hi, **are you ready to order**?

BROTHER: Yes, we are.

SISTER: I **would like** the chicken Caesar salad.

WAITRESS: Anything to drink?

SISTER: Just water **for now.**

WAITRESS: And how about you?

BROTHER: I'll have the same, but I'd also like the vegetable soup.

WAITRESS: **Will that be all?**

BROTHER: Uh-huh. **That's all** for now.

WAITRESS: OK. I'll be right back with your soup.

BROTHER: Thanks.

After You Listen

(A) Below are details about the introductory conversation. Circle the letter of the correct answer, *a* or *b.*

1. a. They don't have time to relax and talk very often.
    b. The brother and sister often have time to relax and talk.

2. a. They are each going to pay for half the lunch.
    b. The brother is going to pay.

3. a. For the brother, this is the first time in this restaurant.
    b. For the brother, this isn't the first time in this restaurant.

4. a. The brother is very shy.
    b. The sister is very shy.

5. a. The sister doesn't want soup.
    b. They are both going to have soup and salad.

(B) Say the conversation in groups of three. Then have three students say the conversation in front of the class.

Work with Others

If you're working with a partner or in a small group, read the short dialogues and examples for each expression aloud. Also, complete the Your Turn exercises together. Then, for each expression, circle *Yes* or *No* to show if you understand. If you circled *No*, highlight or underline what is unclear, and ask questions about what is not clear.

Figure It out on Your Own

Read the short dialogues and examples for each expression. Also complete the Your Turn exercises that don't need partners. Then, for each expression, circle *Yes* or *No* to show if you understand. If you circled *No*, highlight or underline what is still unclear, and ask questions in class about what is not clear.

ALL CLEAR ?
Yes   No

1. **eat óut = go óut to éat** = eat in a restaurant (**past = ate/went**)

   A: Let's **eat out** tonight. I don't want to cook.
   B: We **ate out** last night. I'll make you dinner. What do you want?

   A: Let's do something special for your birthday. Let's **go out to eat.**
   B: Really? That's a great idea! Thank you!

   Similar Expression: **eat outside** = eat in the fresh air, under the sky

   A: Can we **eat outside?**
   B: I don't know. I think it's going to rain.

Your Turn

1. What do you want to do tonight—cook, eat out, order a pizza, or get take-out Chinese food?

2. Do you plan to go out to eat next month to celebrate a special occasion (a birthday, an anniversary)? If yes, where? For what occasion?

3. Do you have a balcony, patio or yard where you can eat outside in nice weather (where you live now and/or in your native country)?

2. **tréat (someone) to (something)** = pay for someone (for example, for a meal or for a movie)

A: It's your birthday. I want to **treat you** to the movie.
B: Thank you, but it's too expensive. I can pay for my own ticket.
A: No, I'm happy to do it. It's your birthday present.
B: Wow! Really? Thank you!

Similar Expression: **It's mý tréat!**

A: Put away your wallet. **It's my treat!**
B: No. Let's split the bill (you pay half and I pay half).
A: No. You just graduated and I want to **treat you.**
B: That's really nice. Thank you. But please let me leave the tip.

Culture Note

When someone offers to treat you, it is common to first say 'No,' and then to accept. What is the custom in your native country?

Your Turn

Work with a partner. Choose a special occasion from the list. Then use one of the dialogues above as a model for your conversation.

Special Occasions:
a birthday
a graduation
a celebration because one person just came back after a long time
a going-away lunch for one person who is going to be away for a long time
Other: _____

3. **ónce in a whíle** = sometimes

Note: Once in a while can be an answer to the question, "How often. . . ?"

A: How often do you come to this restaurant?
B: Oh, **once in a while.** When I want to celebrate something special.

A: Do you speak English when you're not in class?
B: Do I speak English when I'm not in class? Hmm. That's a very interesting question. Well, I have to say I speak English only **once in a while** because we don't speak English at home. But I watch TV a lot.

Your Turn

Circle your answers. Then compare yourself to your partner.

1. How often do you read the newspaper?	Every day	Once in a while	Never
2. How often do you clean your room?	Every day	Once in a while	Never
3. Do you study a lot?	Every day	Once in a while	Never
4. Do you try to use new expressions when you speak English?	Every day	Once in a while	Never
5. When you listen to people speak English, do you hear them using expressions you studied?	Every day	Once in a while	Never
6. How often do you _____?	Every day	Once in a while	Never

ALL CLEAR ?

4. whatéver you wánt = you can have or do anything that you want

A: The party's at 8 o'clock.
B: Can I wear jeans?
A: Sure. You can wear **whatever you want.**

Similar Expressions: **wheréver you wánt** = in any place that you want
whenéver you wánt = at any time that you want

A: Where do you want to eat?
B: **Wherever you want.**
A: Really? How about that new Chinese restaurant near your house?
B: Great idea! What time do you want to go?
A: **Whenever you want.**

Your Turn: Listening Challenge

Listen to Speaker A. Choose the best response for Speaker B: *a, b,* or *c.*

1. (a) Whatever you want.   (b) Wherever you want.   (c) Whenever you want.
2. (a) Whatever you want.   (b) Wherever you want.   (c) Whenever you want.
3. (a) Whatever you want.   (b) Wherever you want.   (c) Whenever you want.
4. (a) Whatever you want.   (b) Wherever you want.   (c) Whenever you want.
5. (a) Whatever you want.   (b) Wherever you want.   (c) Whenever you want.

I,22

5. **I'll háve** = I would líke to órder . . . (I'd líke to órder . . .)

   A: Can I take your order?
   B: Yes. I think **I'll have** a cheese omelette.
   A: With toast or a muffin?
   B: Toast. And my son **will have** scrambled eggs with toast.
   A: Anything to drink?
   B: Yes. **I'll have** coffee and **he'll have** orange juice.

ALL CLEAR ?

Yes   No

Pronunciation:
- I'll = 'eye' + 'ul'
- soup or salad = "supersalad"

Your Turn

The dialogue above is about ordering breakfast. Using that dialogue as an example, work with a partner and order lunch for yourself and your friend.

A: Can I take your order?

B: Yes. I _____.

A: With soup or salad?

B: _____. And my friend _____.

A: Anything to drink?

B: _____.

6. **be hungry**—Use this expression when you want to eat.

    Note: When you use this expression, be sure to use the verb *be*.

HUNGRY

ANGRY

A: Mom, I**'m hungry!**
B: Well, dinner isn't ready. Here's a carrot for you.

A: You ate a lot tonight.
B: I know. I **was** very **hungry.**

Similar Expressions: **I'm stárving** = I'm very, very, very hungry.
                          I'm thírsty = I need something to drink.

- Let's get something to eat. **I'm starving** because I didn't have breakfast.
- Can you wait for me? I need to get some water because I**'m** very **thirsty.**

Your Turn

Write a short dialogue. You are at school and you forgot your lunch. What do you say to your friend?

A: _____

B: _____

7. **Are you réady to órder?** = **Can I táke your órder?** = Please tell me what you'd like to eat. **We're réady to órder.** = We know what we want to eat.

    A: Hi. **Are you ready to order?** (Can I take your order?)
    B: Uh, I think we need a few more minutes to look at the menu.
    A: No problem. I'll come back in a few minutes.

A: Excuse me. **We're ready to order.**

B: I'll be right there.

Culture Note

In the United States, you can call a waiter or waitress by making eye contact and saying, "We're ready to order." To catch the waiter or waitress' eye, you can raise your hand just a little bit.

Your Turn

How do you get the waiter's or waitress' attention in a restaurant in your native country?

___ (a) wave your hand   ___ (d) make a sound

___ (b) catch his or her eye   ___ (e) Other: _____

___ (c) snap your fingers

8. **would líke** = "I would like. . ." is a polite way to say "I want . . ."

ALL CLEAR ?

Notes:

• When you order in a restaurant, you can say "I would like" or "I'll have."

Contractions with *would:*

I would = I'd like   she would = she'd like
you would = you'd like   we would = we'd like
he would = he'd like   they would = they'd like

Question Form: **What would you like?** = What do you want?

                       Would you like . . . ? = Do you want . . . ?

Pronunciation: The *l* in *would* is silent. Don't say the *l.*

A: Hi. Are you ready to order?

B: Uh-huh. **I'd like** the fish special.

A: And **what would you like?**

C: I'll have the spaghetti.

A: **Would you like** soup or salad with that?

C: Salad. With oil and vinegar.

A: **Would you like** more coffee?

B: Sure. Thanks a lot.

Your Turn

You and your partner are at a restaurant. Your partner doesn't know any English, so you have to order the food for him or her. First, each of you chooses one item from each column of the menu below. Then order for both of you.

```
                          MENU
__ chicken and rice    __ french fries    __ coffee
__ a tuna sandwich     __ onion rings     __ tea
__ a hamburger         __ onion soup      __ orange juice
__ a cheeseburger      __ a salad         __ sparkling water
```

A: Are you ready to order?
B: Yes. I'd like _____.
   And my friend would like _____.

9. **for nów** = for the moment (temporarily)

   A: Can I get you anything else?
   B: No, thanks. I'm fine **for now.** (But maybe later I will want something else.)

   A: Where do they live?
   B: Well, **for now** they live in the city, but when they have children, they'll move.

   • I know we have a lot to talk about, but **for now,** let's just talk about these expressions.
   • My car is OK **for now,** but I know that it's getting old.
   • This is enough **for now,** but maybe we'll order dessert later.

Your Turn

Finish these sentences.

1. I'm studying English for now, but later I will _____.

2. _____ is the President of the United States for now, but later he (she?) will have to find another job.

3. _____ is my partner in class for now, but next week or next month I will have a new partner.

10. **Will thát be áll? = Is thát ít?** = You don't want anything else?
    Thát's áll. = Thát's ít. = We don't want anything else.

    Note: Notice the answers to these questions:

    A: Will that be all?   A: Is that it?
    B: Yes, that's all.   B: Yes, that's it.

A: OK. You want one hamburger, one cheeseburger, and two orders of fries. **Will that be all?** (Is that it?)

B: Uh-huh. **That's all.** (That's it.)

Your Turn

Look at the Your Turn Section in Number 8. Add "Will that be all?" and "Yes, that's all" to the dialogue.

NEW EXPRESSION COLLECTION

eat out	whatever you want	I would like . . .
go out to eat	I'll have . . .	for now
treat someone to something	be hungry	That's all.
once in a while	ready to order	That's it.

Exercises

(See page 164 for pronunciation exercises for Lesson 5.)

1. Mini-Dialogues

I,23

Read the sentences in Column A. Choose the *best* response from Column B. To check this exercise, say each mini-dialogue with a partner. One student will read a line from Column A, and another student will answer with a line from Column B.

1A	1B
___ 1. Are you ready to order?	a. Great idea!
___ 2. How often do you eat here?	b. Not yet. We need another minute.
___ 3. It's my treat.	c. Whenever you want.
___ 4. Where do you want to eat?	d. No thanks. I'm fine for now.
___ 5. Let's go out to eat.	e. Once in a while.
___ 6. Can I get you anything else?	f. Oh, no. Thank you. But I'll pay half.
___ 7. When do want to leave?	g. Wherever you want.

2A	2B
___ 1. What are you going to have?	a. No, thanks. I'm fine.
___ 2. Would you like some more coffee?	b. Where did you go?
___ 3. We ate outside last night.	c. Whatever you want.
___ 4. We ate out last night.	d. Was it cold?
___ 5. I'm so thirsty.	e. I'm not very hungry. I think I'll just have a cup of soup.
___ 6. Will that be all?	f. Why don't you ask for some water?
___ 7. Dad, what kind of drink can I get?	g. Yes, that's all.

2. Grammar Practice

Follow the directions and complete the sentences.

Directions	Sentences
1. Use past tense.	a. We (eat) _____ out last Saturday.
	b. We (negative: eat) _____ out last Sunday.
	c. They (go) _____ out to eat.
	d. We (negative: go) _____ out to eat.
2. Add a preposition.	a. I was surprised when they treated me _____ dinner.
	b. We don't eat out often. We eat out once _____ a while.
	c. We're happy living here _____ now, but I think we'll move in a year or two.
3. Add a contraction.	a. Put your wallet away. _____ my treat!
	b. Excuse me. _____ like to order.
	c. Excuse me. _____ ready to order.
	d. _____ have a salad, and _____ have a tuna sandwich.
	e. _____ hungry and thirsty.

3. Error Correction

Find the errors and make corrections. Every item has *one* mistake.

1. We eat out once a while.

2. We didn't ate out last night.

3. I have thirsty.

4. I can't believe it. They treat me to dinner last week.

5. They go out eat every Wednesday. It's expensive!

6. A: Are you ready to order?

   B: Yes, I have the chicken.

7. A: Will that be all?

   B: Yes, it's all.

4. Listen and Write the Expressions

The brother and sister from the introductory dialogue are eating out again. It is about six months later, and the sister is treating her brother to lunch for his birthday.

As you listen, fill in the blanks with the expressions that you hear. When you finish, perform the conversation with two classmates.

BROTHER: Now I can thank you. You know I love to (1) _____. And this is a great birthday present.

SISTER: Well, I'm just glad to (2) _____ you and have time to sit and talk with you. Life these days is so busy . . .

WAITER: Hi! (3) _____?

SISTER: I'm sorry. We need a few more minutes.

WAITER: No problem. I'll come back.

BROTHER: So, what are you going to have?

SISTER: I don't know, but I want you to order (4) _____.

BROTHER: I have to tell you, I (5) _____ . . .

SISTER: That's OK. It's your birthday and you can have anything. Hmm . . . I think (6) _____ the fish special. It sounds really good.

BROTHER: You know, I think (7) _____ the same thing.

SISTER: Where's the waiter? . . . Oh, there he is . . . Excuse me. (8) _____.

WAITER: (9) _____?

SISTER: (10) _____ the fish special.

WAITER: With soup or salad?

SISTER: Salad. With oil and vinegar on the side, please.

WAITER: And how about you?

When you get salad dressing "on the side," *you* put the dressing on the salad.

BROTHER:	I'll have the same.
WAITER:	OK. That's two fish specials and two salads with oil and vinegar on the side. (11) _____?
SISTER:	Yes, that's all (12) _____. Thanks.

5. Sentence Writing

Write sentences or mini-dialogues with expressions from this lesson. Use the New Expression Collection list on page 91.

6. Dictation

I,25

You will hear the dictation three times. First, just listen. Second, as you listen, write the dictation on a piece of paper. Skip lines. Third, check what you wrote. *Key Words:* kind, turkey, sandwich

After the dictation, proofread. Circle your mistakes. Don't erase them. Think about what you need to study.

WAITRESS: _____
_____

CUSTOMER: _____
_____

WAITRESS: _____
_____

CUSTOMER: _____
_____

WAITRESS: _____
_____

CUSTOMER: _____
_____

WAITRESS: _____
_____

CUSTOMER: _____
_____

7. Walk and Talk—*Find Someone Who . . .*

A. Walk around the room and ask about five of your classmates the following questions: What is your favorite kind of appetizer? Soup? Salad? Main course? Dessert? Beverage?

Write short answers in the chart on page 95. You don't need to write students' names.

Favorite Kinds of				
Appetizers	Soups and Salads	Main Courses	Desserts	Beverages

B. After you get the information, get into a group of three or four students. Imagine that you are all going to open a new international restaurant together. Give your restaurant a name, and use the information in the chart above to make a menu. Add to the menu if you wish. Decide on the prices you will charge.

_____
(name of restaurant)

Appetizers $ **Soups** $
-
-
-

Salads $ **Main Courses** $
-    • Today's Special: _____
-    •
-    •

Desserts $ **Beverages** $
-    •
-    •

C. Alone or with a partner, write a paragraph on a piece of paper about the restaurant that your group will open. Give the name of the restaurant and talk about some of the kinds of food that you will serve. Also, give the price range of the main courses (for example, main courses will cost from $3 to $10). Use the future tense.

We plan to open an international restaurant. We will name the restaurant

_____

8. Role Play

Choose three or four students to be waiters and waitresses. They will each have four copies of the menus they made in Exercise 7B on page 95.

Do the following:

- On the board, write: the name of the restaurant
                                                expressions listed on page 91

- Choose three or four groups of students to each sit at a group of desks. These will be the tables at the restaurant. (If there are more students in the class, they can join the tables or listen and watch.)

- The waiters and waitresses will each have a table to serve. They will give menus to the customers. The customers will order lunch or dinner.
- Try to use as many of the new expressions as possible. If you can, bring in tablecloths, cups, plates, etc.

Possible first lines:
How are you today? Here are the menus. I'll be back in a few minutes to take your order.

Possible way to end:
Excuse me. Can we have the check, please?

Additional Role Play

Three of you are eating at a restaurant, but you are all having a terrible time. Your waiter or waitress brings the wrong food. One order is not cooked enough. One of you spills water all over the table. And one of you drops your fork on the floor. There are even more problems . . .

9. Write a Dialogue

Write a restaurant conversation on your own or with a partner.
Give the people in the cartoon names, and use at least five of
the expressions below.

Start with *"The restaurant is so crowded!"*
(Also, try to use some expressions from other
lessons that you studied.)

eat out	be thirsty
I'll have	for now
be hungry	whatever you want
Will that be all?	Are you ready to order?
It's my treat!	once in a while
I'd like	eat outside

10. Word Search

Complete the underlined expressions. Then find the complete expressions in the puzzle. The
words can be spelled backwards. They can also be vertical (↕), horizontal (↔), or diagonal (↗) (↖).

1. We can eat _____ you want—
    near home or in the city.

2. They're buying some bottles of water
    because they _____ thirsty.

3. We had a picnic yesterday. We
    _____ outside.

4. Our refrigerator is empty. Let's
    go _____ to eat.

5. A: Would you like anything else?
    B: No thanks. That's all
    for _____ .

6. A: OK. Eggs and toast. Is that it?
    B: Yes, _____ it.

7. Excuse me. We're ready _____ .

8. Hmm. I think I'll _____
    a salad.

9. Hmm. _____ like the
    chocolate cake. We're going to share it.

```
T N A W U O Y R E V E R E H W
J I W E D L I K E P Q H U K G
T A E O T T U O O G M T D Z S
G U M U C S Y Q A I F K K S C
U B F V B S Z Y T T P C W G R
A N O V K W S C E V V R K Y M
R C R C H D G G O A T J U P U
E C N D I E V E U I H C Y R B
T I O J Y H S J T N A Q V R C
H K W N W V D J S E T E U Z F
I Y Y D E C V P I Y S A R E D
R T K T C X U T D L I E T O O
S W T O P Z G C E T T K B W I
T M R E D R O O T Y D A E R Z
Y U T T I G I L L H A V E C H
```

11. Make a Speech—Appendix C

Prepare a five minute speech about one of the following topics. (See Appendix C on page 177 for more information.) Talk about one of these things:

- A special birthday celebration in my family
- An experience that I had in a restaurant
- My experience as a waiter/waitress

12. Hot Seat—Appendix D

Interview a classmate. Choose one student to come to the "Hot Seat" (a chair) in the front of the room. Or, get into groups and choose one student in each group to be on the "Hot Seat." This student will answer questions. See Appendix D on page 182 for sample questions. It is best to *not* ask personal questions.

My Leg Is Killing Me!

Theme: Talking About Your Health

Warm-Up

Answer these questions with a partner or small group.

1. Did you ever break a bone? If yes, what happened? Who helped you?

2. What sound do people make in your native language when they get hurt?

   English: Ow! or Ouch!

   Your native language: _____

Focused Listening

Before You Listen

Look at the cartoon above. What happened to Mike? What do you think Judy is saying to him? What do you think they will do?

I,26

As You Listen

(A) Close your book. Listen to the conversation between Mike and Judy to find the answers to these questions.

Why did Mike fall down?   What is Judy going to do?

(B) Listen again, but this time, read the conversation as you listen.

MIKE: Ow. My leg **is killing me.**

JUDY: **What happened?**

MIKE: I was coming down the stairs too fast and I **fell down.**

JUDY: Do you think your leg is broken?

MIKE: I don't know, but **it hurts** a lot.

JUDY: Maybe you need to go to the emergency room.

MIKE: No, let's wait a few minutes and see if it gets better.

JUDY: OK. But can I get you anything?

MIKE: Hmm . . . Maybe some ice.

JUDY: OK. I'll **be right back** . . . OK, here. Can you move your leg?

MIKE: **I think so.** But look — it's **getting swollen.**

JUDY: Listen Mike. I'm calling an ambulance **right away. Stay put** and don't move.

After You Listen

(A) Answer these questions with short *yes* or *no* answers. Use *is, are, does, did* and *can* (and their negative forms if necessary). Check your answers with a partner.

1. Did Mike go down the stairs too fast? _____

2. Does his right leg hurt? _____

3. Does his left leg hurt? _____

4. Does Mike want to go to the emergency room immediately? _____

5. Can Mike move his right leg? _____

6. Is Judy going to call an ambulance? _____

7. Are they worried? _____

(B) Say the conversation in pairs. Then have two students say the conversation in front of the class.

Understanding the New Expressions

Work with Others

If you're working with a partner or in a small group, read the short dialogues and examples for each expression aloud. Also, complete the Your Turn exercises together. Then, for each expression, circle *Yes* or *No* to show if you understand. If you circled *No,* highlight or underline what is unclear, and ask questions about what is not clear.

Figure It out on Your Own

Read the short dialogues and examples for each expression. Also complete the Your Turn exercises that don't need partners. Then, for each expression, circle *Yes* or *No* to show if you understand. If you circled *No,* highlight or underline what is still unclear, and ask questions in class about what is not clear.

1. **be killing someone**—You say this when a part of your body hurts very, very much. It does not mean that anyone is being killed.

   A: My head is **killing me.**
   B: Why don't you take some aspirin?
   A: I don't have any. Do you?
   B: Uh-huh. Here. Take two. I'll get you some water.
   A: Thanks a lot.

   A: Where's Rick?
   B: His tooth is **killing him,** so he went to the dentist.

ALL CLEAR ?

Yes   No

Take
- medicine
- a pill
- aspirin

Your Turn

Complain to your partner that something really hurts. Your partner will try to help you by giving you ideas about how you can get better:

YOU:	Oh, my _____ is killing me.
YOUR PARTNER:	Why don't you _____?

ALL CLEAR ?

Yes No

2. **Whát háppened?**—Ask this question when you want to know what occurred.

A: **What happened?**
B: I can't find my wallet.
A: Uh-oh. Let me help you look for it.

A: I was absent this morning. Can you tell me **what happened** in class?
B: Sure. We worked in groups and then we had a quiz.

Your Turn

Tell another student that you were absent for the last class. Ask him or her to tell you what happened in class that day. He or she may need to look at the textbook and at notes to remember. Use the second dialogue above as a model.

Contrast: **Whát's háppening? = Whát's going ón?** (right now)

A: Hi Roberto. **What's happening?**
B: Nothing special (*OR:* Not much). Same old routine.

A: Hi Roberta. **What's happening?**
B: Oh, I've been really busy at work. But everything's OK.

ALL CLEAR ?

Yes No

3. **fall dówn**—accidentally go from standing to the floor or ground (**past = fell**)

Notes:

(1) Usually we don't put words after "fall down." We just say "I fell down." But we can say *where* we fell down: "I fell down the stairs." We can also say "I fell down *and* broke my leg."

(2) Be careful with the past tense. The past of *fall* is *fell*. The past of *feel* is *felt*.

- There's ice on the ground, and you need to be careful or you'll **fall down.**

A: Why is he crying?

B: He **fell down** and hurt his knee.

Similar Expressions: **fall óff** (something)/**fall óut** (**of** something)

on ≠ off
in ≠ out (of)

Note: If something is ON something like a table, it can FALL OFF. If something is IN something like a pocket, it can FALL OUT (OF something).

- The book was on the table. When the earthquake hit, the book **fell off** (the table).
- His keys were in his pocket. When he was jogging, his keys **fell out** (**of** his pocket).

A: What happened during the earthquake?

B: I stayed under a table and things **fell off** bookshelves and they **fell out of** kitchen cabinets. I was scared.

Your Turn

Fill in the blanks with *fell off, fell out of,* or *fell down*. All of these sentences are in the past tense.

During the earthquake,

1. The plate was ON the table.   it fell OFF the table.

2. The picture was ON the wall.   it _____ the wall.

3. The book was ON the shelf.   it _____ the shelf.

4. *Your example:*

   _____   _____

When she was running,

5. Her keys were IN her pocket.   her keys _____
   her pocket.

6. A book was IN her backpack.   a book _____
   her backpack.

7. Her wallet was IN her purse.   her wallet _____
   her purse.

8. *Your example:*

   _____   _____

9. The ice skater _____ three times last night. Ouch!

10. The baby _____ a lot when he was learning to walk.

11. During the earthquake, many people _____.

12. *Your example:* _____

ALL CLEAR ?
Yes   No

4. will be ríght báck = will return immediately

A: Oh, I forgot my wallet. I**'ll be right back.**
B: I'll wait here.

A: Where's Judy?
B: She**'ll be right back.** She went to get some ice.

My Leg is Killing Me!

Your Turn

Complete these dialogues.

A: Where's _____?

B: He'll be right back. He _____.

A: Where are _____?

B: They _____. They'll be right back.

5. **I thínk só./I dón't thínk só.**—These expressions can be answers to *yes-no* questions that ask for information. Say these expressions when you are not 100 percent sure (certain).

ALL CLEAR ?

A: Is she sleeping?
B: **I think so.** I'll go check . . . Yes, she's asleep. (*OR:* No, she's awake.)

A: Do we have a test today?
B: **I think so** . . . Let me see . . . Uh-huh. That's right. The teacher said Tuesday.

A: Is his leg broken?
B: **I don't think so,** but he needs to have an X-ray so we can be sure.

A: Are they coming to the party tonight?
B: **I don't think so.** They said they were probably going to stay home.

Note: You can say "Yes, I think so" or "No, I don't think so" to give your *opinion* when someone asks, "Do you think . . . ?"

A: Do you think we should leave early?
B: Yeah, **I think so.** There's going to be a lot of traffic.

A: Do you think English is easy?
B: No, **I don't think so.**

> *Pronunciation:* To make the voiceless "th" sound, put your tongue between your front teeth and blow air. Put your hand in front of your mouth to feel the air. Don't be afraid to have your tongue out a little bit. If your tongue is in, you will make the /t/ or /s/ sound, not the "th."

My Leg is Killing Me! 105

Your Turn

Ask your partner the following questions about Mike and Judy from the introductory conversation. Your partner will answer with "I think so" or "I don't think so."

Questions	Answers
1. Do you think Judy is Mike's mother?	_____
2. Do you think Mike has a broken leg?	_____
3. Did Mike and Judy go to the hospital?	_____
4. Did Mike go to work the next day?	_____
5. Do you think Mike will be more careful on the stairs next time?	_____

ALL CLEAR ?

6. **(it) húrts**—You can say something *hurts* when you feel pain in parts of your body. **(past = hurt)**

A: How's your leg?
B: **It hurts** a lot, so I can't walk.

A: You look better today. How's your leg?
B: Thanks. **It hurt** a lot yesterday, but today I'm feeling better.

Pronunciation:

• *Ache* is pronounced "ake" as in "make."
• Stress the first word in noun compounds. (The stressed parts of the words are in capital letters.)

My head		I have a HEADache.
My stomach		I have a STOMACHache.
My tooth	hurts.	I have a TOOTHache.
My back		I have a BACKache.
My ear		I have an EARache.

Your Turn: Listening Challenge

Listen to the man complain. He has a lot of problems. Tell him what to do to feel better.

1,27

Your Advice:

1. You should _____.
2. You should _____.
3. You should _____.
4. You should _____.
5. You should _____.

7. **gét/be swóllen**—When a part of the body gets bigger because you get hurt or because you break a bone, it gets "swollen."

ALL CLEAR ?

A: How's your leg, Mike?

B: **It's getting swollen.** I think I need some ice.

A: How's your leg now, Mike?

B: It hurts and **it's swollen.** I think I need to see a doctor.

A: How's your leg now, Mike?

B: It's much better. It **was swollen** yesterday, but today it's better.

Note: When you have the flu, it is common to **have swollen glands**:

A: What's wrong? You look sick.

B: I am. I **have swollen glands** and a sore throat.

Your Turn

These are problems when you have a cold or have the flu:

When you have <u>a</u> cold, you:

sneeze

cough (*gh* is pronounced like an *f*)

When you have <u>the</u> flu, you can:

have a fever

sneeze

cough

have a sore throat

have swollen glands

have an upset stomach

Talk about the last time you had a cold or the flu. How did you feel? What medicine did you take?

ALL CLEAR ?

Yes   No

8. ríght awáy = immediately

A: Mom, can you come home? I feel sick.

B: What's wrong?

A: I have a sore throat, and I think I have a fever.

B: I'll be there **right away.**

A: Is dinner ready? I'm hungry.

B: It'll be ready **right away.** Why don't you set the table?

Your Turn

Complete the three conversations.

(a) Mother: _____
     Child: I'll be there right away.

(b) Child: _____
     Mother: I'll be there right away.

(c) Person: _____
     Police: We'll be there right away.

9. **stáy pút** = stay where you are; don't go anywhere

A: I need to go to work.
B: No, you don't. You have the flu. Just **stay put** and don't go anywhere. Take care of yourself.

• We moved two times in five years. I don't want to move anymore. I want to **stay put.**

Your Turn

Complete this dialogue. There is a big storm outside. What does Speaker B say to Speaker A?

A: Let's go to the movies.
B: _____

NEW EXPRESSION COLLECTION		
killing me	fall off	it hurts
What happened?	fall out of	be/get swollen
What's happening?	will be right back	right away
fall down	I (don't) think so.	stay put

Exercises

I, 28

(See page 166 for pronunciation exercises for Lesson 6.)

1. Mini-Dialogues

Read the sentences in Column A. Choose the *best* response from Column B. To check this exercise, say each mini-dialogue with a partner. One student will read a line from Column A, and another student will answer with a line from Column B.

1A	1B
___ 1. Mama! I fell down! Aah!	**a.** Nope. We're going to stay put and relax at home.
___ 2. Are you going anywhere this weekend?	**b.** I think so, but I'm not sure.
___ 3. Oh, my back is killing me.	**c.** He fell down the stairs and broke his leg.
___ 4. Are Judy and Mike married?	**d.** Maybe you're working at your computer too much.
___ 5. What happened to Mike?	**e.** Come over here and let me look at your knee.
___ 6. Hi Judy! What's happening?	**f.** Not much. Just the same old routine.

Nope is a friendly way to say *No*.

2A	2B
___ 1. Where are you going? We have to leave right away.	**a.** I'll be right back. Don't worry.
___ 2. Look! My wrist is getting swollen.	**b.** I broke my leg.
___ 3. My favorite cup fell off the table and broke.	**c.** I'll get you another one.
___ 4. What happened? Why are you on crutches?	**d.** You're right. Do you think you broke it?
___ 5. Do you think they'll get married?	**e.** No, I don't think so.

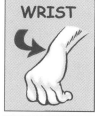

WRIST

CRUTCHES

110 | My Leg is Killing Me!

2. Grammar Practice

Follow the directions and complete the sentences.

	Directions	Sentences
1.	Use past tense.	a. The baby (fall) _____ down and cried. b. His leg doesn't hurt now, but it (hurt) _____ a lot last week. c. It (negative: hurt) _____ last month.
2.	Add *down, of, off.*	a. Her phone fell out _____ her pocket. b. His books fell _____ his desk. c. The picture fell _____ and he picked it up.

3.	Complete the dialogues with expressions from this lesson.	a. A: _____?
		   B: Nothing much. How about you?
		b. A: _____? Why do you look so happy?
		   B: We just decided to get married!
		c. A: Is there a test today?
		   B: _____.
		d. A: _____ and don't go anywhere.
		   I'll _____.
		   B: OK. But please be quick.

3. Error Correction

Find the errors and make corrections. Every item has *one* mistake.

1. I lost my dictionary. I think it fell out my backpack.

2. Be careful. Your glass is going to fall down the table.

3. The shelf in my closet is completely full. When I opened the door, everything on the shelf felt down.

4. Stay put. I will right back.

5. His knee is get swollen. He needs some ice.

6. A: Why is she walking like that?

   B: She hurts her back yesterday.

4. Listen and Write the Expressions

The following is a conversation between Mike, Judy and a doctor. They are at a hospital emergency room. As you listen, fill in the blanks with the expressions that you hear. When you finish, perform the conversation with two classmates.

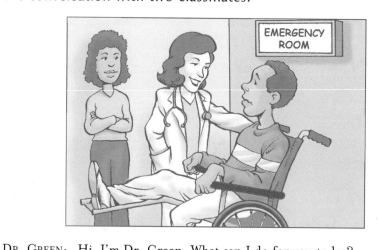

DR. GREEN: Hi, I'm Dr. Green. What can I do for you today?

MIKE: My leg (1) _____. I think I broke it.

DR. GREEN: (2) _____?

MIKE: I (3) _____ the stairs. I was reading something and I wasn't paying attention . . .

DR. GREEN: Hmm. That's how these things happen. Here, let me take a look . . . Well, your leg (4) _____.

MIKE: And I put ice on it.

DR. GREEN: You need to get an X-ray (5) _____. Wait here a moment and (6) _____.

(a few minutes later)

DR. GREEN: Excuse me, what's your name?

JUDY: Judy.

DR. GREEN: OK, Judy, take Mike down the hall to room 212 for his X- ray. Then go back to the waiting room and I'll call you.

JUDY: Thanks, Dr. Green. Do you think his leg's broken?

DR. GREEN: (7) _____, but I want to be sure.

JUDY: OK. Thanks, doctor. Let's go, Mike.

5. Sentence Writing

Write sentences or mini-dialogues with expressions from this lesson. Use the New Expression Collection list on page 110.

6. Dictation

You will hear the dictation three times. First, just listen. Second, as you listen, write the dictation on a piece of paper. Skip lines. Third, check what you wrote. *Key Words:* top, stairs, hospital, broken

After the dictation, proofread. Circle your mistakes. Don't erase them. Think about what you need to study.

I,30

7. Walk and Talk—BINGO

(A) Ask the *Yes-No* questions on the BINGO card. Walk around the classroom and ask your questions. When a student says "Yes, I do" or "Sometimes" write his or her first name in the box. The first person to get five names in a straight line [vertical (↑), horizontal (↔), or diagonal (↗) (↖)] is the winner.

Example:
A: *Do you take vitamins?*
B: *No, I don't.*
A: *OK. Thank you.*

A: *Do you take vitamins?*
B: *Yes, I do.*
A: *Great! What's your first name?*
. . . How do you spell it?

Do you go to the doctor for a check-up once a year?	When you have a cold, do you take aspirin?	When you have the flu, do you drink tea?	When you have a sore throat, do you go to the doctor right away?	Do you usually have swollen glands when you have a cold?
Do you take vitamins every day?	Do you cover your nose when you sneeze?	Do you say something when a person sneezes?	Do you take medicine when you have a fever?	Do you take medicine when you have an upset stomach?
Do you stay home from work when you have a cold?	Do you have a headache right now?	Free Space	If you see a person fall down, do you laugh?	If you see a person fall down, do you help?
If your tooth is killing you, do you go to the dentist?	Did you break a bone when you were younger?	Did you fall down a lot when you were a child?	Did you have earaches when you were a child?	Do (Did) your grandparents have different ideas about kinds of medicine to take?
If your friend needs your help, do you help him or her right away?	If money falls out of someone's pocket, do you pick it up and return it?	Do you think chicken soup is good when you have a cold?	Do you have a thermometer at home?	Do you eat a lot of fruit and vegetables?

(B) Write sentences about what five students told you in Exercise 7A. After you finish, show the sentences to those students to make sure that your information is correct.

8. Role Play

Imagine that your classroom is a doctor's office. Choose students for the following roles:

- doctor
- medical assistant
- receptionist
- four adult patients
- one mother or father with a child

The five patients all have different problems:

- Mike has a broken leg (Judy may be with him.)
- someone has the flu (with fever, coughing, sneezing, sore throat, swollen glands)
- someone has a cold (with sneezing and coughing)
- someone has a stomachache
- the child has an earache (his or her parent is very worried)

Each patient comes in one at a time and goes to the receptionist. The receptionist gets the person's name and asks the patient to sit down or "take a seat." Then the receptionist gives the list of names to the medical assistant.

After all of the patients are sitting in the waiting room, the medical assistant comes out and asks for the first patient. Each patient goes in to see the doctor and medical assistant and tells them what the problem is. When they finish, they leave and the next patient goes in. The doctor and medical assistant ask a lot of questions and help the patients.

Here are some expressions that you can try to use. They can be
written on the board.

___ is killing me	have a(n) ___ache	I don't think so
have swollen glands	have a fever	have a cold
get/be swollen	I fell down	have the flu
right away	I think so	have a sore throat

Possible starting lines:

RECEPTIONIST: *Hi. Can I help you?*

PATIENT: *Yes, I have an appointment with Dr. _____.*

RECEPTIONIST: *What's your name?*

PATIENT: _____

RECEPTIONIST: *OK. Please have a seat.*

9. Write a Dialogue

Work on your own or with a partner. Write a conversation between a
doctor and one of the patients from Exercise 8. Give the patient a
name, and use at least five of the expressions below.

Start with the doctor saying, *"So, how are you today?"* (Also, try to use
some expressions from other lessons that you studied.)

is killing me	What happened?	fall down	have a(n) ___ache
it hurts	will be right back	I think so	I don't think so
stay put	right away	have a cold	have the flu
fall out of			

10. Tic-Tac-Toe

In tic-tac-toe, to get an *X* or an *O* in a space, you need to make a
sentence that is correct in grammar and meaning. Here is a game with
expressions from Lesson 6. (See page 55 for more detailed directions.)

fall down	**fall off**	**fall out of**
right away	**stay put**	**___ hurts**
is swollen	**will be right back**	**___ is killing me because**

11. Make a Speech—Appendix C

Prepare a five minute speech about one of the following topics. (See Appendix C on page 177 for more information.) Talk about one of these things:

- A medical experience someone had
- What people in my native country do when they have the cold or flu
- What food is necessary for good nutrition
- How exercise helps us have good health

12. Hot Seat—Appendix D

Interview a classmate. Choose one student to come to the "Hot Seat" (a chair) in the front of the room. Or, get into groups and choose one student in each group to be on the "Hot Seat." This student will answer questions. See Appendix D on page 182 for sample questions. It is best to *not* ask personal questions.

Collocation Match-Up

Collocations are special combinations of words. Collocations can be idioms or other phrases and expressions. Find collocations from *Lessons 5* and *6* by matching the words from Column A with the words in Column B. Sometimes more than one answer is possible. (You will probably be able to make additional expressions that are not from Lessons 5 and 6. Put these in the box.)

A

1. for _____
2. fall off _____
3. fall out of _____
4. fall _____
5. I don't _____
6. once _____
7. What would _____
8. Will that _____
9. It's _____
10. go out _____
11. Are you ready _____
12. whenever _____
13. Is that _____
14. stay _____
15. eat _____
16. right _____
17. It _____
18. We're ready _____
19. be _____
20. I'll be _____

B

in a while

thirsty

you want

to order?

to order.

you like?

now

out

be all?

to eat

the table

his pocket

right back.

think so.

it?

hurts

away

put

down

my treat!

Additional Collocations

Crossword Puzzle

Across

3 He's absent because he ___ a bad cold.

6 I'd ___ soup and a salad.

7 The glass fell ___ the table and broke.

8 My head ___. Do you have any aspirin?

11 Stay ___. Don't move. I'll be right back.

14 My feet ___ because I walked far in bad shoes.

16 You can do ___ you want.

18 You look worried. What ___?

20 What ___ you like to eat?

21 Ow! My back is ___ me!

Down

1 She has ___ flu so she's absent today.

2 Sit down. I'll bring you water ___ away.

4 I don't think ___.

5 The little boy fell out ___ a tree and broke his arm.

9 Excuse me. We're ___ to order.

10 He got a ___ after he ate all that candy.

12 You can go ___ you want.

13 We ___ very hungry tonight.

15 The baby ___ down and cried.

17 We go to the movies once in a ___.

19 We're fine for ___.

20 ___ that be all?

Shopping for Jeans

**Theme: Shopping and
Giving Compliments**

Warm-Up

Answer these questions with a partner or in a small group.

1. Imagine that you have a free afternoon. What will you do? Why?

____ a. take a nap (sleep)

____ b. relax and watch TV

____ c. relax and read

____ d. go to a movie

____ e. exercise

____ f. go shopping

____ g. visit friends

____ h. other: _____

2. Do you like to go shopping for food? for clothes? Why or why not?

3. Do you shop at flea markets? farmer's markets? Why or why not?

Before You Listen

Look at the cartoons on page 119. What do you think the salesperson is saying in the first cartoon? What do you think the woman is saying in the second cartoon?

As You Listen

2,1

(A) Close your book. Listen to the conversation in the store to find the answers to these questions.

What do Lynn and Jim ask the salesperson?   Does Jim buy a pair of jeans?

(B) Listen again, but this time, read the conversation as you listen.

SALESPERSON:	Can I help you?
LYNN:	Thanks, **we're just looking.**
SALESPERSON:	Well, **let me know** if there's anything I can do for you.
	* * * * *
JIM:	**What do you think of** these jeans?
LYNN:	They're really nice. **How much** are they?
JIM:	Hmm . . . there's no price tag. Where's the salesperson? I'm going to ask her . . . Oh, there she is. Excuse me, **how much** are these jeans?
SALESPERSON:	I'll be with you in a minute . . . . OK. Let's see. They were $29, but I think today they're 30 percent off. Yes, that's right. They're about $20. That's a good price for these jeans.
JIM:	Can I **try them on?**
SALESPERSON:	Sure. The fitting rooms are right **over there.** Just **go on in.**
JIM:	Thanks a lot.
	* * * * *
JIM:	Pssst. Lynn, how do they look?
LYNN:	Oh, Jim! They're too big. I'll get you a smaller size . . . Wait a minute . . . Here, try these.
	* * * * *
JIM:	I think these are better. How do they look?
LYNN:	They're perfect.
SALESPERSON:	Oh, they look very nice on you.
JIM:	Great. **I'll take** them.

After You Listen

(A) Below are details about the introductory conversation. Circle *T* for *true*, *F* for *false*, or *?* if you don't know.

1.	Jim and Lynn are married.	T	F	?
2.	The salesperson is helpful.	T	F	?
3.	They found jeans that are the right size for Jim.	T	F	?
4.	The jeans aren't on sale today.	T	F	?
5.	Next, they're going to look for jeans for Lynn.	T	F	?

(B) Say the conversation in groups of three. Then have three students say the conversation in front of the class.

Understanding the New Expressions

Work with Others

If you're working with a partner or in a small group, read the short dialogues and examples for each expression aloud. Also, complete the Your Turn exercises together. Then, for each expression, circle *Yes* or *No* to show if you understand. If you circled *No*, highlight or underline what is unclear, and ask about what is not clear.

Figure It out on Your Own

Read the short dialogues and examples for each expression. Also complete the Your Turn exercises that don't need partners. Then, for each expression, circle *Yes* or *No* to show if you understand. If you circled *No*, highlight or underline what is still unclear, and ask questions in class about what is not clear.

1. **I'm júst lóoking./We're júst lóoking.**—You can say this to a salesperson if you don't want help when you are shopping.

   A: Hi. Can I help you?
   B: Thanks. **I'm just looking.** (We're just looking.)
   A: Fine. Let me know if you need any help.
   B: I will.

ALL CLEAR ?

Yes   No

Your Turn

Say the dialogue above with a partner.

Pronunciation: In "I'll let you know," the last sound in "I'll" is *l* and the first sound in *let* is also 'l'. Don't say the 'l' two times. Pronounce *I'll let* as one word.

2. **lét (me, you, him, her, us, them) knów** = tell (me) later

Grammar Note: This expression is usually in two forms:

- imperative (command): (Please) let me know!
- future tense: I'll let you know (later).

A: Did she have a girl or a boy?
B: I don't know. I'm going to call them right now.
A: Please **let me know** as soon as you can.
B: OK. I'll call you right away.

A: This homework is really hard.
B: **Let me know** if you need my help.

A: Do you want to go shopping tomorrow?
B: I'm not sure yet. I'll **let you know** tonight.

A: They need to know where the party is.
B: I'll **let them know.**

Your Turn

Finish the sentences on the right. Use *"let . . . know."*

1. I need to know what time the movie starts.

   I'll let you know later.

2. They want to know if they passed the test.

   The teacher will _____.

3. When is the party?

   I'll _____.

4. Can you come on Friday night?

   I'm not sure. I'll _____.

5. I'm sorry. I don't know when I can visit you.

   No problem. Just _____ when you have time.

3. **Whát do you think of . . . ?** = Whát is your opínion of . . . ?

A: **What do you think of** classical music?
B: I like it a lot. But I like rock music better.

A: **What do you think of** this watch?
B: It's nice, but it's too expensive.

A: **What do you think of** American food?
B: Hmm. That's a difficult question.

Your Turn

Ask your partner for his or her opinion.

Questions	Answers (use adjectives)
What do you think of American food?	I think it's _____.
English?	_____
classical music?	_____
rock music?	_____
_____	_____

4. **Hów múch are thése (jéans)?/Hów múch is thís (shírt)?** = How much
   money does this cost?

   Grammar Note: Say "How much are *these*?" if you are asking about a plural
   noun. Use "How much is *this*?" if you are asking about a singular noun.

   Nouns that are always plural:

	clothes	shorts
	jeans	pajamas
	pants	glasses

   A: Excuse me. **How much are these** sunglasses?
   B: I'm not sure. I'll check.

   A: **How much is this** jacket?
   B: Let's see . . . It's $60.

   Contrast: **How much are they? How much is it?**—Use *they* and *it* after
   someone makes a statement about specific items. *They* and *it* are pronouns.

   A: These shoes are nice.   A: That's a nice watch.
   B: **How much are they?**   B: **How much is it?**

ALL CLEAR ?

Yes   No

Your Turn

1. On the left is a list of things in a department store. On the right, write
   questions to ask to get the price. Use *this* or *these*.

Things to buy	Questions to ask a salesperson
1. table	How much _____?
2. earrings	_____
3. boots	_____
4. sweater	_____

2. Complete these dialogues. Use *it* or *they*.

   A: Wow! I love this ring.   A: _____
   B: <u>How much</u> ____?   B: _____

5. try (something) ón = put on clothes or shoes to see if they fit (if they are the right size) and to see if they look nice

FITTING ROOM

A: I really like this <u>shirt</u>.
B: Why don't you **try it on?**   (Use *it* for the singular word, *shirt*.)

A: I really like these <u>jeans</u>.
B: Why don't you **try them on?**   (Use *them* for the plural word, *jeans*.)

You can just use *this* or *these* when you and the person you are talking to both see what you are talking about.

A: Excuse me. Where can I **try this on?**
   (*this*—singular)
B: The fitting room is right over there.

A: Excuse me. Where can I **try these on?** (*these*—plural)
B: The fitting room is right over there.

2,2

Your Turn: Listening Challenge

Listen to the sentences. Add to what each person is saying. Fill in the blanks with *it* or *them*.

1. Where can I try _____ on?

2. I'm going to try _____ on.

3. I'm sorry I didn't try _____ on before I bought it!

4. Can I try _____ on?

5. I tried _____ on.

6. **(be) (gó) over thére**—This is a place that is not near you. It is not here. It is common to say **ríght over thére** or **gó over thére.**

Note: Use *come* with "here" and *go* with "there."

A: Excuse me. Where's the teacher?
B: She's **right over there.**
A: Oh, I see her. Thanks.

A: Where's my book?
B: Maybe it's at Lynn's house. Remember—you studied with her yesterday.
A: Oh, that's right! I need to **go over there** right now and get it because I need to do my homework.

Similar Expression: **(be) (cóme) over hére**

A: Where are you?
B: I'm **over here.** Under the car.

A: Dad, I fell and my leg hurts.
B: **Come over here** and let me look at it.

Your Turn

On the right, write *over there* or *over here.*

1. He's with me.　　　　　He's _____.

2. He's across the street.　　He's _____.

7. gó on ín—This is a friendly way to tell someone to go into something that is "over there."

A: Is the restaurant open?
B: Uh-huh. **Go on in.**

A: Don't wait for me. I'll park the car. You **go on in.**
B: OK. We'll see you inside.

Similar Expression: **Cóme on ín** = friendly way to say "Come in."

Note: You say "Come on in" when you want someone to come into a place where you are. You say "Go on in" when you want someone to go into a place, but you are not there.

A: Hi, you guys! **Come on in.** It's great to see you!
B: Thanks. It's great to be here.

Your Turn

On the right, write *come on in* or *go on in*.

1. I'll be right there. Don't wait for me. _____.

2. Welcome! _____

8. Hów do they lóok?/Hów does it lóok?/They lóok . . . /It lóoks . . . (+ adjective)—You can ask people these questions when you try clothes on. You ask these questions if you want their opinion. They will tell you if the clothes "look good on you."

A: What do you think of these shoes? **How do they look?**
B: **They look** really nice. Are they comfortable?

A: What do you think of this jacket? **How does it look?**
B: I think it's too long.

Your Turn

Get a picture from a magazine or newspaper. Write down at least three things the person or people are wearing. Then write a question and answer for each item.

What they are wearing	Questions	Answers (use adjectives)
Example:		
a necklace	How does it look?	It looks beautiful.
earrings	How do they look?	They look beautiful.
_____	_____	_____
_____	_____	_____
_____	_____	_____
_____	_____	_____

9. **I'll (We'll) táke . . . .** —You can say this to a salesperson in a store when you are ready to buy something.

ALL CLEAR ?

A: Hi. Do you want to take this sweater?
B: Yes. **I'll take it.**

A: Hi. We're ready. **We'll take** this chair.
B: OK. I'll be right with you.

A: Hi. **I'll take** these jeans.
B: Will that be all? (Do you want anything else?)
A: Yes, that's all.

Your Turn

Work with a partner. Put some items (books, pens, wallets, purses, earrings, jackets, etc.) on a desk. One student can be the salesperson and the other student can be the customer. Think about singular and plural, and follow this sample dialogue.

A: Can I help you?
B: Yes. I'll take this _____ or I'll take these _____.
A: Will that be all?
B: Yes, that's all.

Exercises

(See page 167 for pronunciation exercises for Lesson 7.)

1. Mini-Dialogues

Read the sentences in Column A. Choose the *best* response from Column B. To check this exercise, say each mini-dialogue with a partner. One student will read a line from Column A, and another student will answer with a line from Column B.

1A	1B
___ 1. Can I help you?	a. Yeah, but how much is it?
___ 2. What do you think of this suit?	b. Yeah, but how much are they?
___ 3. Excuse me. Where can I try this on?	c. It's nice. But how much is it?
___ 4. Are those new jeans?	d. Over there, in the fitting rooms.
___ 5. These are great sunglasses.	e. Uh-huh. How do they look?
___ 6. That's a great watch.	f. I'm not sure. Can I let you know later?
___ 7. Can you come over tonight?	g. Thanks. I'm just looking.
___ 8. Hi. Are you busy?	h. No. Come on in!

2,3

2. Grammar Practice

Follow the directions and complete the sentences.

	Directions	Sentences

I.	Complete these sentences and questions with *try on.*	a. I like these pants. I'm going to _____.
		b. A: I need to return these jeans because they're too small.
		   B: Didn't you _____ before you bought them?
		c. A: Are you going to buy the green shirt?
		   B: I don't know. I need to _____.
		d. A: Where is she?
		   B: She's _____ a lot of clothes.
		e. A: Why are you so unhappy?
		   B: I _____ about five pairs of pants, and none of them fit me!

2.	Add *this* or *these.*	a. How much are _____ shoes? b. How do _____ shoes look? c. What do you think of _____ coat? d. I'll take _____ jeans. e. How much is _____ backpack?

3.	Complete the questions with *How much.* Use *it* or *they.*	a. A: These are nice shoes.
		   B: How much _____?
		b. A: Mom, can we get that backpack?
		   B: Is it expensive? How much _____?

3. Error Correction

Find the errors and make corrections. Every item has *one* mistake.

1. (Talking to someone at school) It's 3:30. I need to come home right away.

2. (Talking at home) I come to school at 9:00 every morning.

3. (Talking in the United States) When I come back to my native country, I will see my family.

4. These shoes are really comfortable. I'll take it.

5. I just got new glasses. What do you think them?

6. I like your glasses. Can I try on them?

7. I didn't try the jeans, and now I have to return them.

8. How these glasses look on me?

9. How does this shirt looks on me?

10. Thanks. We just looking.

11. How much this is?

12. How much is these?

4. Listen and Write the Expressions

The following is a conversation between Lynn, Jim, and a salesperson. Lynn and Jim finished shopping for jeans, and now they are shopping for a wedding gown for Lynn. (A wedding gown is a special dress for a woman who is getting married.)

As you listen, fill in the blanks with the expressions that you hear. When you finish, perform the conversation with two classmates.

SALESPERSON: Hello. How are you two today?

LYNN: Fine, thanks.

SALESPERSON: Can I help you find a wedding gown?

LYNN: Thanks, but (1) _____ right now.

SALESPERSON: No problem. (2) _____ if I can help.

JIM: Thanks. Lynn . . . look at this one. (3) _____ this?

LYNN: It's beautiful. (4) _____?

JIM: It's too expensive.

LYNN: Come on . . . Tell me how much . . .

JIM: Two hundred.

LYNN: (to the salesperson) Excuse me. Can I (5) _____?

SALESPERSON: Sure. The fitting rooms are right (6) _____.

   Just (7) _____.

LYNN: Thanks . . . . Jim . . . I'm ready . . . (8) _____?

JIM: Wow! You look fantastic!

SALESPERSON: Yes, it looks beautiful on you.

LYNN: (9) _____. But Jim, please don't wear your new jeans to our wedding!

130   Shopping for Jeans

5. Sentence Writing

Write sentences or mini-dialogues with expressions from this lesson. Use the New Expression Collection list on page 128.

6. Dictation

You will hear the dictation three times. First, just listen. Second, as you listen, write the dictation on a piece of paper. Skip lines. Third, check what you wrote.

2,5

Key Words: Lynn, Jim, $200, laughs, salesperson, wedding gown

After the dictation, proofread. Circle your mistakes. Don't erase them. Think about what you need to study.

7. Walk and Talk

1. Set up a department store in your classroom. Bring in things to sell. Set up the following departments.

Departments	What Can You Bring to Class?
• men's department	_____
• women's department	_____
• shoes	_____
• jewelry	_____
• wallets, purses	_____
• other: _____	_____

Choose students to be salespeople in the different departments. These students should:

- make signs that say "_____ Department"
- arrange the items they are selling
- decide on the prices and make price tags to put on each item (Remember, prices in a department store can't be changed.)

The other students are the shoppers. Each student will shop with a partner.

Everyone should try to use some of the expressions from this lesson. To help you remember them, you can write the list from page 128 on the board.

2. Write five sentences about what you did in the Walk and Talk activity. For example, if you were a salesperson, you can write, *I sold jeans to three people.* If you were a shopper, you can write, *I tried jeans on.*

- _____
- _____
- _____
- _____
- _____

8. Info Gap — Flea Market

Imagine that two people are talking at a flea market. At a flea market, people can talk about changing the prices. This is called bargaining. You cannot do this in a department store.

One person (Speaker 1) is selling many different things, and the other person (Speaker 2) is a shopper.

Work with a partner. One of you will be Speaker 1 and the other will be Speaker 2. Speaker 1 will look at page 175 and Speaker 2 will look at page 176. You will have different information to give each other. Don't look at your partner's page.

Variation: All students who are Speaker 1 can set up tables or desks around the classroom. All students who are Speaker 2 can walk around the room and go shopping.

When you finish:

1. The shoppers will tell the class what they bought.
    Examples of what they can say:
    - I bought _____ because _____.
    - The seller wanted $20, but I paid $__.

2. The sellers will tell the class what they sold.
    Examples of what they can say:
    - I sold _____.
    - The customer wanted to pay only $10, but we bargained, and I got $12.

9. Write a Dialogue

Work on your own or with a partner. Write a conversation between Sam and Jack. Use at least five of the expressions from the box.

Start with Sam saying *"Jack, look . . ."* (Also, try to use some expressions from other lessons that you studied.)

What do you think of . . . ?	How much are . . . ?
How much is . . . ?	How do . . . look?
How does . . . look?	over here
try . . . on	over there

10. Unscramble and Find the Secret Message

Unscramble the words and write them in the puzzle. Then find the secret message at the bottom of the page.

ROEV EETRH

CEMO ON IN.

I'LL AKTE TEHES NSJEA.

TWAH OD YOU ITNKH OF SHTI?

EW'RE UJST LIKGONO.

I ETDRI HTEM NO.

GO ON NI.

TLE EM KNOW.

WOH CMHU ARE THYE?

OWH UCHM IS STHI?

WOH OD HYET OLKO?

OWH DSEO IT OLOK?

11. Make a Speech—Appendix C

Prepare a five minute speech about one of the following topics. (See Appendix C on page 177 for more information.) Talk about one of these things:

- The advantages and disadvantages of shopping online
- How to bargain at a flea market
- How to plan and organize a yard sale

12. Hot Seat—Appendix D

Interview a classmate. Choose one student to come to the "Hot Seat" (a chair) in the front of the room. Or, get into groups and choose one student in each group to be on the "Hot Seat." This student will answer questions. See Appendix D on page 182 for sample questions. It is best to *not* ask personal questions.

Who's Cooking Tonight?

Theme: Male
and Female Roles

Warm-Up

Answer these questions with a partner or in a small group.

1. Do you know anyone who works at home (not in an office)?

   __ Yes __ No   If yes, who? _____

   What kind of work does he or she do? _____

2. In your family, who usually

   • cooks dinner?   _____

   • washes the dishes?   _____

   • does the laundry?   _____

3. Is it common in your native country for men to do any of the things
   in number 2?

   __ Yes __ No

   Explain.

Before You Listen

Look at the cartoon on page 137. A woman is talking to her husband. What do you think she is saying?

As You Listen

2,6

(A) Close your book. Listen to the conversation between the husband and wife to find the answers to these questions.

Why is she late?   Who took a nap?

(B) Listen again, but this time, read the conversation as you listen.

HUSBAND:	Hello.
WIFE:	Honey? It's me . . .
HUSBAND:	Where are you?
WIFE:	At the station. I **missed my train** so I'm going to be late.
HUSBAND:	Oh, that's too bad. Will you **get back in time to** pick up the kids?
WIFE:	I don't think so. Can you get them?
HUSBAND:	**No problem.**
WIFE:	**Make sure** they start their homework.
HUSBAND:	Don't worry. What time do you think you'll be home?
WIFE:	Probably in about an hour. How was your day?
HUSBAND:	Well, I worked for a few hours at the computer, and then I **got sleepy,** so I **took a nap.**
WIFE:	You took a nap! You're so lucky you work at home. I can't take a nap in the office, you know.
HUSBAND:	But I also **did the laundry** and **the dishes.** You can't do those things at the office.
WIFE:	Well, that's true. Hey, what's for dinner?
HUSBAND:	Chicken. It'll be ready when you **get home.**
WIFE:	**I can't wait.** I love your chicken.
HUSBAND:	And I love *you.* See you around 6:30?
WIFE:	I hope so. See ya.

After You Listen

(A) Below are details about the introductory conversation. Circle *H* for what the husband does, did, or is going to do. Circle *W* for what the wife does, did, or is going to do.

1.	is going to pick up the kids	H	W
2.	works in an office	H	W
3.	works at home	H	W
4.	commutes to work	H	W
5.	will make sure the kids do their homework	H	W
6.	took a nap	H	W
7.	did the laundry and the dishes	H	W

(B) Say the conversation in pairs. Then have two students say the conversation in front of the class.

Understanding the New Expressions

Work with Others

If you're working with a partner or in a small group, read the short dialogues and examples for each expression aloud. Also, complete the Your Turn exercises together. Then, for each expression, circle *Yes* or *No* to show if you understand. If you circled *No*, highlight or underline what is unclear, and ask about what is not clear.

Figure It out on Your Own

Read the short dialogues and examples for each expression. Also complete the Your Turn exercises that don't need partners. Then, for each expression, circle *Yes* or *No* to show if you understand. If you circled *No*, highlight or underline what is still unclear, and ask questions in class about what is not clear.

1. **míss (my/the) tráin/bús** = not get on a train or bus because you arrive late at the station or bus stop

   - Oops! I have to leave now. I don't want to **miss my train.**
   - She **misses the bus** every day. She needs to get up earlier.
   - I'm sorry I'm late. I **missed the bus.**

   Other things you can miss: an appointment, a party, a class, a test, etc.

ALL CLEAR ?

Who's Cooking Tonight? | 139

Note: **Miss** has another meaning. You can *miss* a person because you are not together. You can *miss* a place because you are not there. You can *miss* things because you don't have them right now.

- I **miss** my family. I'm homesick and I want to go back.
- He **misses** his native country and his mother's cooking.

Your Turn

1. Describe what happened when you missed something (a bus, a train, a plane, an appointment, a party, a class, a test, etc.).

2. Talk about a person, place, or thing that you miss right now.

ALL CLEAR ?
Yes No

2. **get báck** – arrive at the place you started from (return) **(past = got)**

   A: I'm going shopping.
   B: What time will you **get back?**
   A: Probably around 2:00.

   - I'm sorry I didn't call you. I **got back** late.

   Note: **Back** is not a verb. It is *not* correct to say: I'll back later.

Your Turn

Complete the dialogues.

   A: The party is going to start at 8:00.
   B: Don't worry. I _____ by 7:00.

   A: Are they on vacation?
   B: No, they _____ yesterday.

ALL CLEAR ?
Yes No

3. **in tíme to (*do* something) / in tíme for (something)** = before it is too late
   Use *get to a place* with **in time to** + verb:
   Don't worry. I'll get home **in time to** *eat* dinner.
                                                  drive you to work.
                                                  watch the movie with you.
                                                  help you with your homework.

   Use *get to a place* with **in time for** + noun:
   I'm sorry. I can't get home **in time for** dinner.
                                                     the movie.
                                                     the party.

   Contrast:

   - They didn't get to school **in time to** take the test.
   - They didn't get to school **in time for** the test.

Your Turn

Fill in the blanks with *to* or *for*.

1. I'm so happy. Last night I got home in time _____ see you on TV.

2. We were late. We didn't get there in time _____ buy tickets, so we didn't see the movie.

3. He is going to be late for the birthday party. But I hope he will be in time _____ the cake.

Similar Expression: **on tíme** = punctual, when something is expected

- Don't be late. Come **on time.**
- I know the party starts at 8:00, but tell him that it starts at 7:00 because he's never **on time.**

4. nó próblem—say this when someone asks you to do something, and you are happy to do it. It means "yes," but it is more friendly.

A: Can you help me carry these bags?
B: Sure. **No problem.**

A: Is it OK if we go to the movies on Sunday? I'm busy on Saturday.
B: **No problem.**

ALL CLEAR ?

Your Turn

Complete this dialogue.

A: _____?
B: No problem.

5. máke súre = make certain/definite **(past = made)**

- It's raining. **Make sure** you take your umbrella.
- The party is a surprise. **Make sure** you don't tell her about it.
- I think the plane leaves at 10:00, but I'll check my ticket to **make sure.**
- Don't worry. I **made sure** the door is locked.

ALL CLEAR ?

Your Turn

Tell someone to *make sure* about something.

1. We have a test next week. _____

2. The bus leaves at 7:45. _____

3. We need milk. _____

4. _____ _____

6. **gét sléepy =** You become tired and then feel like you can sleep. Your eyes are heavy and you yawn. **(past = got)**

- When students **get sleepy** and they need to study, they often drink coffee.
- After driving for five hours, the driver **got sleepy,** so he stopped at a hotel.

A: How was the movie?

B: Not very interesting. It was really boring. I **got sleepy** and wanted to go home.

Contrast: "sleepy" and "sleeping"

Words	Part of speech	Meaning
She is *sleepy.*	adjective	She is tired and she needs to sleep.
She is *sleeping.*	verb	She is sleeping. She is not awake. She is asleep.
She is *asleep.*	adjective	She is sleeping.
She is *awake.*	adjective	She is not sleeping.

Your Turn

Answer the questions with a partner or group.

What do you do when you get sleepy and you are:

- driving? _____

- in class? _____

- studying for a test? _____

7. **táke a náp** = sleep for a short time, usually in the daytime **(plural: take naps) (past = took)**

ALL CLEAR ?

A: I'm tired. I think I'm going to **take a nap.**
B: Sweet dreams!

A: Shh! The baby **is taking a nap.**
B: Sorry. I didn't know.

A: You look great!
B: Thanks. I **took a** two-hour **nap** this afternoon, and now I have a lot of energy.

> **Culture Note**
>
> In some cultures, people take naps or have a "siesta" in the afternoon. Is that common in your native country?

Your Turn

Conduct a survey on naps. Interview five classmates and take short notes in the chart.

Question: *Do you like to take naps?*

Classmate	**Yes** • When do you take naps? • How do you feel after a nap?	**No** Why don't you like to take naps?
1.		
2.		
3.		
4.		
5.		

8. **dó (the) (my) láundry** = wash the clothes **(past = did)**

- (Present continuous tense for *right now*)
  I'm really busy now. **I'm doing the laundry** and cleaning the house.
- (Past tense for *yesterday*)
  I was busy yesterday. **I did the laundry** and cleaned the house.
- (Present tense for *every* Saturday-routine)
  Every Saturday, I **do my laundry.**
  you **do your laundry.**
  he **does his laundry.**
  she **does her laundry.**
  we **do our laundry.**
  they **do their laundry.**
- (Future tense for *next week*)
  I did your laundry today. **Will** you **do my laundry** next week?

Your Turn

Answer the questions with a partner or in a small group.

1. Who does the laundry in your family?

2. In your opinion, is it OK for men to do the laundry?

3. If you do your laundry, where do you do it?
   ___ At home?   ___ At a laundromat?

4. Do you like to do your laundry?   ___ Yes   ___ No
   Why or why not?

9. **dó the díshes** = wash the dishes

A: I cooked dinner, so you need to **do the dishes.**
B: OK. I'll do them later.

A: I **did the dishes** last night, so you need to do them tonight.
B: But I'm so tired.
A: That's OK. It will only take you about ten minutes.

Answer the questions with a partner or in a small group.

1. Who does the dishes in your family?

2. In your opinion, is it OK for men to do the dishes?

3. Do you have a dishwasher? ___ Yes ___ No

   If yes, who "loads" (puts dirty dishes in) and "unloads" (takes clean dishes out of) the dishwasher?

10. **gét hóme** = arrive at home

   (past = got)

ALL CLEAR ?

get home
early
late
at 2:00
around 3:30
about 7:00
on time
in time for dinner
in time to eat

A: What time do you usually **get home** from work every day?
B: Oh, usually about 5:30. But if there's a lot of traffic, I **get home** around 6:00.

A: You look tired.
B: I am. I **got home** very late last night.

A: Did you watch the special on Channel 9 last night?
B: No, I **didn't get home** in time and I forgot to record it.

Your Turn

Ask three students the following question: *What time do you usually get home every day?* Then write sentences about each student. Use the students' names.

1. _____ usually gets home _____.

2. _____

3. _____

11. **cán't wáit (to/for)** = want something good to happen very soon **(past = couldn't)**

ALL CLEAR ?

- They're getting married next month, and they **can't wait.**
- Tomorrow is payday (the day she gets paid at work), and she **can't wait to** get her check.
- She **can't wait for** her check.
- She was really excited about her new job, and she **couldn't wait** to tell her friends about it.

Note: Use *can't wait* **to** + verb. Use *can't wait* **for** + noun.

can't wait to	can't wait for
He can't wait *to have* his birthday party.	He can't wait *for* his birthday party.
She can't wait *to get* her paycheck.	She can't wait *for* her paycheck.
I can't wait *to have* my vacation.	I can't wait *for* my vacation.
They couldn't wait *to get* married.	They couldn't wait *for* the wedding.

Your Turn

On the left, write three things that you can't wait *to do,* and on the right, write three things that you can't wait *for:*

I can't wait to

_____

_____

_____

I can't wait for

_____

_____

_____

2,7

Your Turn: Listening Challenge

Listen to the people talk about what they *can't wait to do* and what they *can't wait for.* Put a check (√) next to the items that they talk about.

_____ a vacation   _____ food   _____ a grade   _____ a baby

_____ a concert   _____ a test   _____ a party   _____ a new car

_____ a TV show   _____ a parent

ALL CLEAR ?

12. **(I) hópe só.** = I want that to happen.

A: Are you going to learn English quickly?   B: **I hope so.**

A: Are you going to be there on Saturday?
B: **We hope so.** We have to go somewhere first, but we'll try.

Opposite: (I) **hópe nót.** = I don't want that to happen.

A: Is it going to rain?   B: **I hope not!** We want to go to the beach.

A: Do we have a test today?   B: **I hope not!** I didn't study.

Your Turn

Finish these short dialogues.

A: _____ ?
B: I hope so.
A: _____ ?
B: I hope not.

NEW EXPRESSION COLLECTION		
miss something	make sure	get home
get back	get sleepy	can't wait to/for
in time to/for	take a nap	I hope so.
on time	do the laundry	I hope not.
no problem	do the dishes	

Exercises   *(See page 169 for pronunciation exercises for Lesson 8.)*

1. Mini-Dialogues

Read the sentences in Column A. Choose the *best* response from
Column B. To check this exercise, say each mini-dialogue with a partner.
One student will read a line from Column A, and another student will
answer with a line from Column B.

2,8

1A	1B
___ **1.** I'm getting really sleepy.	**a.** I did the laundry and the dishes, and I cleaned the house and worked in the garden.
___ **2.** I hope you locked the door and closed the windows.	**b.** I don't know. I hope so.
___ **3.** Why are you so tired?	**c.** I hope not.
___ **4.** Does he like his new job?	**d.** Why don't you take a nap?
___ **5.** His party is going to be great.	**e.** Don't worry. I made sure everything was OK before I left.
___ **6.** Is she angry with you?	**f.** I know. I can't wait to go.

2A	2B
___ **1.** Why are you in a hurry?	**a.** Don't worry. I'm never late!
___ **2.** What time do you think you'll get home tonight?	**b.** I know there was a lot of traffic.
___ **3.** Can you help me with my homework?	**c.** No problem. I'm happy to help you.
___ **4.** Sorry I got back so late.	**d.** I need to get back in time to make dinner.
___ **5.** Please make sure you're on time for your appointment.	**e.** We'll save you some food.
___ **6.** I'm sorry I won't be home in time for dinner.	**f.** Probably around 9:00.

Who's Cooking Tonight?   147

2. Grammar Practice

Follow the directions and complete the sentences.

Directions	Sentences
1. Add *to* or *for*.	a. We got back in time _____ dinner.
	b. They got back in time _____ have lunch.
	c. They couldn't wait _____ eat because they were so hungry.
	d. He can't wait _____ his birthday party.
	e. I hope you're home in time _____ the movie.
2. Use past tense.	a. She (take) _____ a nap before she went out.
	b. He (get) _____ sleepy at the meeting, so he drank some coffee.
	c. We (make) _____ sure that everyone was comfortable.
	d. She (can't) _____ wait to get her first paycheck.
	e. After he (do) _____ the dishes, he (do) _____ the laundry.
	f. They (get) _____ home late so they were very tired.

3. Error Correction

Find the errors and make corrections. Every item has *one* mistake.

1. The baby is getting sleeping. She needs to take a nap.

2. The baby take a nap every afternoon.

3. I took nap for twenty minutes, and now I feel better.

4. We need to be at the theater in time for to the beginning of the movie.

5. We need to be at the theater in time for to see the beginning of the movie.

6. He makes his laundry once a week.

7. I do the dishes last night. Can you do the dishes tonight?

8. They home late last night.

9. She can't wait for to see you.

10. She can't wait for to her birthday party.

4. Listen and Write the Expressions

The husband and wife from the introductory dialogue are talking in their living room after dinner.

As you listen, fill in the blanks with the expressions that you hear. When you finish, perform the conversation with a partner.

2,9

WIFE: That chicken was really good. I'm lucky that I married you. You're a great cook.

HUSBAND: Thanks.

WIFE: And it's great that you (1) _____ and (2) _____.
Did you have time to do your work at the computer?

HUSBAND: Not today, but tomorrow I'll work a lot. Can you (3) _____ _____ (4) _____ pick up the kids and make dinner tomorrow?

WIFE: Sure. (5) _____. I'll try to (6) _____ _____ early. I'll (7) _____ I take an early train. What do you want for dinner?

HUSBAND: Hmm . . . How about your delicious spaghetti?

WIFE: I can do that. And the kids can help me.

HUSBAND: I (8) _____! I can almost taste it now.

WIFE: You know, it's only 8:30, but I'm (9) _____. I had a busy day.

HUSBAND: And you didn't (10) _____ like I did. Maybe it's a good idea to go to bed early tonight.

WIFE: Yeah, but I want to watch some TV first. What's on?

5. Sentence Writing

Write sentences or mini-dialogues with expressions from this lesson. Use the New Expression Collection list on page 147.

6. Dictation

2,10

You will hear the dictation three times. First, just listen. Second, as you listen, write the dictation on a piece of paper. Skip lines. Third, check what you wrote. *Key Words:* wife, husband, chicken, laundry

After the dictation, proofread. Circle your mistakes. Don't erase them. Think about what you need to study.

7. Walk and Talk

1. Walk to the opposite side of the room and ask two different students questions 1 and 2 in the chart. Also, be sure to ask, "Why?" or "Why not?" Take notes in the chart.

Useful phrase: It depends (on) . . .

Questions	Student Name _____	Student Name _____
1. Do you think it's OK for men to do the laundry, do the dishes, and cook?		
2. Do you think it's OK for women to work if they have young children?		

When you finish, put the class results on the board and have the students give reasons why they said *yes, sometimes,* or *no.*

2. Write two sentences about what each student said to you. Use the students' names.

Question 1

1. ____ said it's OK for men to do the laundry because _____

   _____

2. _____

Question 2

1. _____

2. _____

8. Contact Assignment

With a partner, ask two native English speakers the following questions. You can ask people in your school, at a library or store, or in your neighborhood. You don't need to walk up to strangers on the street.

Introduce yourself like this. You can practice saying this in class:

Hi. We're from _____ and _____ and we're studying English. We have a homework assignment to ask three short questions about male and female roles and household chores. Do you have a minute to answer our questions?

Advice: Look directly at the people you are talking to and take short notes. Don't just look at your book, and don't let the people read the questions.

I. Do you think it's OK for men to do the laundry, do the dishes, and cook?

Reasons

Person I: ___ Yes ___ Sometimes ___ No _____

Person 2: ___ Yes ___ Sometimes ___ No _____

2. Do you think it's OK for women to work if they have children?

Person I: ___ Yes ___ Sometimes ___ No _____

Person 2: ___ Yes ___ Sometimes ___ No _____

3. (You and your partner write a question to ask.)

_____

Person I: ___ Yes ___ Sometimes ___ No _____

Person 2: ___ Yes ___ Sometimes ___ No _____

After you get the information from the two people, answer these questions.

1. When you said you were studying English and you asked people to talk to you, what did they say? _____

   _____

2. Did the native English speakers understand your questions?

   __ always   __ usually   __ sometimes   __ rarely

3. How much did you understand when the native speakers answered your questions? ____ percent

4. How did you feel when you talked to the two native speakers?

   _____

   _____

5. Which responses were the most interesting? Why?

   _____

   _____

9. Write a Dialogue

Work on your own or with a partner. Write a conversation between the mother and the person on the phone. Use at least five of the expressions from the box.

Start with the mother saying *"What time will you get home?"* (Also, try to use some expressions from other lessons that you studied.)

miss	in time to	in time for	do the laundry	do the dishes
I hope so	I hope not	can't wait to	can't wait for	get sleepy
make sure	no problem	get back	on time	take a nap

10. Word Search

Complete the underlined expressions. Then find the complete expressions in the puzzle. The words can be spelled backwards. They can also be vertical (↕), horizontal (↔), or diagonal (↗) (↖).

```
D  O  T  H  E  D  I  S  H  E  S  D  E  E  X
N  L  Q  X  Y  P  H  I  D  K  R  T  S  E  C
R  U  A  W  E  G  T  Q  C  O  W  O  B  M  S
H  M  N  G  D  W  Q  A  F  E  N  A  R  O  M
V  F  P  C  Y  G  B  T  D  T  S  Y  Y  H  O
H  R  D  K  C  T  I  K  I  D  X  Y  V  T  C
T  M  L  D  O  A  E  M  P  P  V  J  R  O  X
O  Y  Z  G  W  G  E  O  L  U  W  D  R  G  G
Y  G  E  T  T  I  N  G  S  L  E  E  P  Y  Q
P  A  N  A  G  N  I  K  A  T  V  C  V  M  S
W  A  V  L  Z  I  N  T  I  M  E  T  O  G  X
C  E  R  O  F  E  M  I  T  N  I  R  A  M  R
R  O  F  F  H  O  T  T  I  A  W  T  N  A  C
G  J  E  M  A  K  E  S  U  R  E  B  X  O  M
F  Z  M  I  S  S  T  H  E  B  U  S  L  A  I
```

1. Ssh! The baby is _____ <u>a nap.</u>

2. He _____<u>back</u> from school late, and now he's tired.

3. She _____ <u>home</u> early today, so she cooked a nice dinner.

4. _____<u>sure</u> you call me at 2 o'clock!

5. I'm _____<u>sleepy.</u> I think I'll go to bed.

6. We did the laundry, but we didn't _____<u>the dishes.</u>

7. You're always _____<u>time.</u> You're never late.

8. Don't worry. I'll be home <u>in time</u> _____ help you get ready for the party.

9. Don't worry. I'll be home in <u>time</u>_____ the party.

10. The children <u>can't wait</u>_____ the party.

11. The children <u>can't wait</u>_____ get presents.

12. Hurry up! You don't want to _____ <u>bus!</u>

11. Make a Speech—Appendix C

Prepare a five minute speech about one of the following topics. (See Appendix C on page 177 for more information.) Talk about one of these things:

- Male and female roles in my grandparents' house and my house
- How to bring up a boy or girl in today's world
- The life of a typical working woman

12. Hot Seat—Appendix D

Interview a classmate. Choose one student to come to the "Hot Seat" (a chair) in the front of the room. Or, get into groups and choose one student in each group to be on the "Hot Seat." This student will answer questions. See Appendix D on page 182 for sample questions. It is best to *not* ask personal questions.

Collocation Match-Up

Collocations are special combinations of words. Collocations can be idioms or other phrases and expressions. Find collocations from *Lessons 7* and *8* by matching the words from Column A with the words in Column B. Sometimes more than one answer is possible. (You will probably be able to make additional expressions that are not from Lessons 7 and 8. Put these in the box.)

A

1. No _____
2. I hope _____
3. I'll _____
4. try _____
5. get _____
6. get _____
7. do the _____
8. take _____
9. We're _____
10. Let me _____
11. What do you _____
12. Can you wait over _____
13. How much _____
14. Come on _____
15. I can't wait _____
16. I can't wait _____
17. miss _____
18. get back _____
19. in time to _____
20. in time for _____
21. get to school _____
22. Make sure _____

B

just looking.

think of this?

laundry

for the weekend.

to see you.

my class

is this?

problem!

go to my class

home

you do your homework.

a nap

there?

the plane

on time

take it.

sleepy

on

in!

know.

not!

at 7:30

Additional Collocations

Crossword Puzzle

Across

3 You can try them on __ there.

4 Let me __ when you can go to the movies.

7 They __ back at 3:00, and then they go to work.

9 She didn't get home in time __ make dinner.

12 Ssh! The baby is taking a __.

14 These shoes are great. I'll take __.

15 Her husband __ the dishes every night.

17 Thank you. We're just __.

19 Make __ you pick me up at 8:00, OK?

20 I'm very __, so I think I'll go to bed.

Down

1 Will you be home in time __ dinner?

2 I got new shoes. How do they __?

5 A: Is the test going to be hard? B: I hope __.

6 I can't __ to see you!

8 Come over __. I want to tell you something.

10 Make sure you're __ time for your appointment.

11 Every day when she __ home, the dog is happy.

13 Sure I can help you. No __.

16 We __ the bus, so we have to walk.

18 What did you think __ the movie?

Pronunciation

LESSON 1: What's Wrong?

Part 1: Sentence Stress

These are the expressions from this lesson:

WHAT'S WRONG	at the BEGINNING
TAKING THIS CLASS	GET to KNOW
HAVE to	MAKE FRIENDS
be AFRAID of	GET BETTER
DON'T WORRY	HAVE TROUBLE

Notice the words that are not in capital letters. These words are usually not strong or stressed (emphasized):

to   (from the infinitive, for example: have "to talk")
be   (verb "be" and am/is/are/was/were)
of, at (prepositions)
the   (article)

Listen and say each expression listed above. Make the words *to, be, of, at,* and *the* less strong (weaker) than the other words.

2,11

Practice saying the first part of the introductory dialogue. Make the capitalized words stronger than the other words.

ANDY: WHAT'S WRONG, Eric?

ERIC: I'm REALLY NERVOUS. I'm ALWAYS THIS WAY on the FIRST DAY of SCHOOL.

ANDY: You're not the ONLY one. It's HARD for me, TOO. I'm GLAD we're TAKING THIS CLASS TOGETHER.

ERIC: Do you KNOW ANYTHING about the TEACHER?

ANDY: UH-HUH, a LITTLE. SOMEONE TOLD me she GIVES a LOT of HOMEWORK, and you HAVE to TALK a LOT in CLASS.

Part 2: Contractions

Contractions are two words put together to form one word. Native English speakers use many contractions when they speak, and that may be why you sometimes don't understand what you hear.

Here are examples of contractions from this lesson. Practice saying the full forms and the contractions.

Full forms	Contractions
what is	what's
I am	I'm
you are	you're
it is	it's
we are	we're
do not	don't
does not	doesn't
the teacher is	the teacher's
let us	let's

Listen and repeat

2,12

1. What's wrong?

2. I'm glad we're taking this class.

3. You're not the only one.

4. It's hard for me, too.

5. Don't worry.

6. It doesn't get better for me.

7. The teacher's here.

8. Let's talk after class.

Part 3: *Hafta* and *Hasta*

Have to is often pronounced "hafta" and *has to* is often pronounced "hasta."

It is important for you to understand this pronunciation when you listen to English, but you do not have to pronounce *have to* in these ways.

Listen to the dialogue again and notice how contractions and *have to* are pronounced.

Part 1: Stress in Phrasal Verbs

In this lesson, you learned four phrasal verbs: *hold on, hang up, pick up,* and *get off.*
Phrasal verbs are verbs with two or more words.

When you say these words, *stress* the second word. That means *make the second
word stronger:* hold ON/held ON; hang UP/hung UP; pick UP/picked UP;
get OFF/got OFF

Listen and repeat

- Hold ON a minute, and I'll get Sara.
- Alex, when are you going to hang UP?
- Why don't I pick you UP at 7:00?
- My parents are calling me for dinner, and I have to get OFF.

2,13

Part 2: Contractions

Here are examples of contractions from this lesson. Practice saying both the full
forms and the contractions.

Full forms	Contractions	Full forms	Contractions
who is	who's	I am	I'm
it is	it's	cannot	can't
I will	I'll	do not	don't

Listen and repeat

1. Who's this?

2. It's Alex.

3. It's for you.

4. I'll be right there.

5. I'm really sorry.

6. I can't make it on Saturday.

7. Why don't I pick you up?

2,14

Practice

Look at the conversations in Lesson 2 on pages 20 and 30–31.

1. Underline these phrasal verbs: *hold on, hang up, pick up,* and *get off.*

2. Put a stress mark (´) over the second part of each phrasal verb.

3. Circle the contractions.

4. Listen again to the conversations. Repeat what you hear.

Sentence Stress

In Lesson 1, you learned that some words in English (for example, prepositions and articles) are not stressed (not said strongly).

Other words need to be said strongly. These words (such as nouns and adjectives) have a lot of information and need to be strong and clear. To understand which words need to be stressed or not stressed, look at the boxes below and on the next page. Most of the words come from the conversation on page 40.

Usually Stressed*

Nouns	Main verbs	Negative helping verbs	Adjectives
weekend	know	don't	three-day
month	have	won't	next
idea	want		great
beach	go		right
winter	take		good
swimming	do		crowded
walks	read		
plenty	need		
things	relax		
movies	think		
reservation	make		
lots	stay		
places			

Also stressed

- Question words (who, what, where, when, why, how)
- Demonstrative adjectives and pronouns (this, that, these, those)
- Forms of *be* when they are the last word in a sentence (Yes, I *am*.)
- Adverbs (quickly, always, very)
- Negative helping verbs (It *doesn't* cost a lot.)

Usually Not Stressed

Forms of be	Prepositions	Articles	Helping verbs	Pronouns	Conjunctions
am is are was were be	to in on of	a an the	do can will	you we I it	but and or so

PRONUNCIATION AND LISTENING PRACTICE

2,15

- Say the following lines from the conversation on page 40. The stressed words are in capital letters.
- Listen again to the conversation. Repeat after the speakers.

1. You KNOW,
   we HAVE a THREE-DAY WEEKEND
   NEXT MONTH.
   Do you WANT to
   GO AWAY?

2. THAT'S a GREAT IDEA!
   WHERE do you WANT to GO?

3. To the BEACH.

4. The BEACH in WINTER?

5. We DON'T HAVE to
   GO SWIMMING.
   We can TAKE WALKS on the BEACH.

6. But WHAT ELSE can we DO?

7. Oh, THERE are PLENTY of THINGS
   to DO.
   We can READ,
   GO to the MOVIES.
   I NEED to RELAX,
   DON'T YOU?

8. I SURE DO
You're RIGHT.
The BEACH is a GOOD IDEA.
And it WON'T be CROWDED.
Do you THINK
we NEED to MAKE a RESERVATION ANYWHERE?

9. NO, I DON'T THINK SO.
THERE are LOTS of PLACES to STAY.
And they'll be CHEAPER NOW
than they are in the SUMMER.

LESSON 4: Wake Up!

Intonation

In Lessons 1, 2, and 3, you learned that it is important to stress some words in English. This helps people understand what a speaker thinks is important.

Intonation also helps people understand what a speaker thinks is important.

Intonation is the   rising (going up)   and   falling (going down)   speaker's voice. of a

Intonation usually goes

- up on the most important words.

- down at the end of a sentence to show that the sentence is ending.

  I don't   want   to get out of   bed.

- up and then down at the end of a sentence if the last word in the sentence is the most important one. If the last word has only one syllable, that word is said longer.

  I   need   to get   up   now and take a   show   er.

- up and then down at the end of *wh-* (information) questions

  Why did I go to bed so   late   last   night?

- up at the end of *yes-no* questions.

  Don't you have to go to the air   port?

Practice

Step 1: Read the dialogue silently and imagine your voice going up and down. Move your hand up and down to show rising and falling intonation.

Step 2: Say the dialogue with a partner, paying special attention to the rising and falling of your voice.

Step 3: Listen to the dialogue. Do you hear the speakers' voices going up and down?

Step 4: Say the dialogue with a partner again.

2,16

MIKE: Wake up, Tom! Don't you have to go to the airport?

TOM: Yeah, I'll get up in five minutes. I don't want to get out of bed—it's so early.

MIKE: Well, I'm going back to sleep. I hope you won't miss your plane. Have a good trip!

TOM: Thanks. Oh, why did I go to bed so late last night? It's so hard to get up, and it's so cold and dark. But I need to get up now and take a shower. What time is it? Six o'clock? Oh no! I'm a late. I don't have time for a shower. I have to get dressed and get to the airport right away.

Stress and Intonation

1. Review the rules about sentence stress (Lessons 1 and 3) and intonation (Lesson 4).

2. Below is the beginning of the introductory conversation from Lesson 5 on page 82. As you say the conversation with a partner, do the following:
   - Stress the capitalized words—make them longer, stronger, and louder than other words.
   - Make your voice go up and down the way the words appear. Try to read with feeling.

```
                                                    TIME
SISTER:     Oh, it's SO NICE to eat OUT and have
                                                        TOGETHER.


                                 BIRTH
              WHAT a GREAT      DAY
                                     PRESENT!


                          LIKE        ALWAYS
BROTHER:  I'm GLAD you            I'm          HAPPY to TREAT
                              it.


                   LU              THINK      KN
              you to    N    And I was       ING, you    OW, we
                   CH.


                               TIME      SIT    TA
              NEVER REALLY HAVE        to just  and   LK . . .


                                    HO                         PL
SISTER:     And NOW we have TWO    U    And THIS is a REALLY NICE  A
                                 RS!                             CE.


                        ONCE
BROTHER:  Yeah, I COME here       in a
                                      WHILE.
```

SISTER: WHAT are you GOING to   HA
                                                         V
                                                          E?

BROTHER: Um . . . I'm NOT   SURE   YOU   EVER   WA
                                  But   ORDER WHAT   you   N
                                  yet.   T.

                    BIRTH
      It's your
                DAY.

3. Listen to the recorded conversation. Notice which words are stressed and how the speakers' voices go up and down.

4. With a partner, perform the whole conversation between the brother and sister. Give special attention to stress and intonation.

2,17

5. Listen to the recorded restaurant conversation in Exercise 3. Then perform that conversation with two partners.

LESSON 6: My Leg Is Killing Me!

Intonation in Questions

Here are the questions from this lesson's two conversations on pages 100 and 112:

Yes-No Questions

Do you think it's broken?
Can I get you anything?
Can you move your leg?
Do you think his leg's broken?

Information (WH) Questions

What happened?
What can I do for you today?
What's your name?

Yes-No Questions—Rising Intonation

When you ask a *yes-no* question, remember that your voice needs to rise (go up) at the end of the question. (See Lesson 4.) Practice asking the questions below.

1. Do you think it's bro **ken?**

2. Can I get you any **thing?**

3. Can you move your **leg?**

4. Do you think his leg's bro **ken?**

Information (Wh) Questions—Rising/Falling Intonation

When you ask an information question, remember that your voice needs to rise (go up) on the last stressed word, and then fall (go down) at the end of the question. Practice asking the questions below:

If the last stressed word is one syllable, stretch it out (make it longer).

1. What **hap** pened?

2. What can I **do** for you to **day?**

3. What's your a **n** me?

PRONUNCIATION and LISTENING PRACTICE

- These are the questions from the introductory conversations in Lesson 5 on pages 82-83. Practice asking these questions, using the rules for question intonation.

Yes-No Questions

Are you ready to order?
(Do you want) anything to drink?
Will that be all?

Information Questions

What are you going to have?
How about you?

- Listen to the introductory conversations in Lessons 5 and 6, and pay special attention to the intonation used in questions. Then practice repeating these questions as you listen.
- Do the Hot Seat activity in Appendix D. As you ask questions, think about question intonation.

2,18

LESSON 7: Shopping for Jeans

Thought Groups and Rhythm

Look at A and B below. Which shows the best way to say the lines?

__ A   or   __ B

A

SALESCLERK:	(Can I help you?)
LYNN:	(Thanks.) (We're just looking.)
SALESCLERK:	(Well,) (let me know) (if there's anything) (I can do for you.)

B

SALESCLERK:	(Can) (I) (help) (you?)
LYNN:	(Thanks.) (We're) (just) (looking.)
SALESCLERK:	(Well,) (let) (me) (know) (if) (there's) (anything) (I) (can) (do) (for) (you.)

The answer is that *A* is better. People say words in "thought groups" when they speak English. The music (rhythm) of English is not natural if you say each word alone.

Words often in a thought group

- a short sentence
- a natural group of words like an expression
- words that go alone

Example

(Can I help you?)
(let me know), (we're just looking)
(thanks), (well)

Pronunciation 167

PRONUNCIATION and LISTENING PRACTICE

- Say the lines of the introductory conversation in thought groups. The words with the most stress and highest intonation are in capital letters.

Can I HELP you?

——
Thanks, we're just LOOKing.

——
Well,
let me KNOW
if there's ANYthing
I can DO for you.

——
What do you THINK of
these JEANS?

——
They're really NICE.
How much ARE they?

——
Hmm. . .
there's no PRICE tag.
Where's the SALESperson?
I'm going to ASK her. . .
Oh,
THERE she is.
ExCUSE me,
HOW much are
these JEANS?

——
I'll be WITH you
in a MINute.
OK.
Let's SEE.
They WERE 29 dollars,
but I think toDAY
they're 30 percent OFF.
YES,
That's RIGHT.
They're about 20 DOLlars.
That's a good PRICE
for these JEANS.

——
Can I try them ON?

——
SURE.
The FITting rooms
are right over THERE.
Just go on IN.
Thanks a LOT.

——
LYNN,
how do they LOOK?

——
Oh, JIM!
They're too BIG.
I'll get you a SMALLer size. . .
WAIT a minute. . .
HERE,
try THESE.

——
THANKS. . .
YEAH,
I think these are BETter.
How do they LOOK?

——
FINE.
OH,
they look very NICE on you.

——
GREAT.
I'll TAKE them.

- Listen again to the conversation. Repeat after the speakers.
- Perform the introductory conversation in groups of three.
- Look at the conversation in Exercise 3. Put parentheses around thought groups. Think about what words go together naturally. Practice saying this conversation in groups of three.

Stress, Intonation, and Rhythm Review

Listen and repeat the Lesson 8 introductory conversation in thought groups. The syllables and words with the *most* stress are in capital letters. Remember to use rising/falling intonation in statements and *wh*-questions. Use rising intonation in *yes-no* questions.

2,20

HONey? It's ME.

Where ARE you?

At the STAtion.

I MISSED my TRAIN
so I'm GOing to be LATE.

Oh, that's too BAD.
Will you get BACK in TIME
to pick UP the KIDS?

I don't THINK so.
Can YOU get them?

No PROBlem.

Make SURE they START their
HOMEwork.

Don't WORry.
What TIME
do you THINK
you'll be HOME?

PRObably
in about an HOUr.

How was your DAY?

Well,
I WORKED
for a few HOUrs
at the comPUter,
and then I got SLEEPy
so I TOOK a NAP.

You took a NAP!
You're LUCKy
you work at HOME.
I can't take a NAP
at the OFfice,
you KNOW.

But I ALso
did the LAUNdry
and the DISHes.
You CAN'T
do those THINGS
at the OFfice.

THAT'S true.
HEY,
WHAT'S for DINner?

CHICKen.
It'll be READy
when you get HOME.

I can't WAIT.
I LOVE
your CHICKen.

And I
love YOU.
SEE you
by six-THIRty?

I HOPE so.
SEE ya.

Appendices

Appendix A: Dictations (Exercise 6)

Your teacher will put the key words on the board to help you with spelling.

Lesson 1, Page 14

Eric is a student. He is very nervous on the first day of class. He is afraid of talking in front of people. His friend Andy tells him, "Don't worry." She says he will get to know people in the class and make friends.

After class Eric feels better, but Andy is nervous. She is afraid of having a lot of homework. Eric tells Andy that he will help her.

Lesson 2, Page 31

When Alex calls his friend Sara, her sister Anna answers the phone. Anna asks, "Who's this?" and Alex says, "It's Alex." Anna tells her sister, "It's for you!" and Sara comes to the phone.

Alex invites Sara to go to the movies on Friday night. Sara can't make it on Friday, but Saturday is good. But they don't go to the movies. They go to dinner and it's great. They want to go to the same restaurant again, but Sara wants to drive there. She also wants to pay.

Lesson 3, Page 52

Alice and Peter go away for the weekend. They go to the beach. It is winter, so they can't go swimming. But they take walks on the beach and they get plenty of fresh air. On Friday night they go dancing, and on Sunday they go ice skating. They have a good time and are very happy.

Lesson 4, Page 71

Tom has to wake up early to go to the airport. But when his roommate wakes him up, he doesn't want to get up. The room is very cold and dark, and he wants to go back to sleep.

Tom gets up, but he doesn't have time to take a shower. He gets dressed quickly and goes to the airport. He's lucky because he doesn't miss his plane.

Lesson 5, Page 92

WAITRESS: Are you ready to order?

CUSTOMER: Yes. What kind of soup do you have?

WAITRESS: Today we have really good chicken soup.

CUSTOMER: That sounds good. I'd like a cup of soup and a turkey sandwich.

WAITRESS: Would you like anything to drink?

CUSTOMER: Yes, I think I'll have some hot tea.

WAITRESS: Will that be all?

CUSTOMER: Yes, for now. Thanks.

Lesson 6, Page 111

Mike is standing at the top of the stairs. He is reading something. Then he falls down the stairs. His leg hurts a lot. He tells his wife Judy that his leg is killing him.

Judy gets ice for him and then she takes him to the hospital. The doctor says that Mike's leg is broken. Mike isn't happy because he has to stay put. He can't go to work for a few days.

Lesson 7, Page 129

Lynn and Jim go shopping together for jeans. Jim asks Lynn, "What do you think of these jeans?" She likes them, but she asks, "How much are they?" They are about $20. Jim tries them on. When Lynn sees Jim, she laughs because the jeans are very, very big. She gets a different size for Jim and these jeans look very nice on him. Jim tells the salesperson, "I'll take them."

Then they go shopping for a wedding gown for Lynn. They are going to get married very soon.

Lesson 8, Page 146

A woman is coming home late from work because she missed her train. She has a cell phone, so she calls her husband and tells him she is late. He will pick up the kids and have a chicken dinner ready when she gets home.

The wife thinks her husband is lucky because he works at home and he can take naps when he gets sleepy. He says that he does the laundry and the dishes because he is home. They have an interesting life.

Lesson 3, Page 54

For Speaker 1

1. Here is information about YOUR summer. You will give this information to Speaker 2 when she or he asks you questions. You will sometimes need to add the words *Yes* and *No*.

   My summer was great.
   I went away for two weeks.
   I stayed with cousins.
   I had a great time.
   I went swimming.
   I played soccer.
   I read two books.
   Sometimes I took long walks on the beach.

2. After you finish giving information about your summer to Speaker 2, ask him/her the following questions, and complete this chart. Just write short notes on the right. Don't try to write every word that Speaker 2 says.

Questions to ask Speaker 2	Information from Speaker 2
How was your summer?	_____
Did you go away?	_____
What did you do on weekends?	_____
Did you have a good time?	_____
What else did you do?	_____
Do you want to go away next summer?	_____
Why?	_____

For Speaker 2

1. Ask Speaker 1 the following questions and complete this chart. Just write short notes on the right. Don't try to write every word that Speaker 1 says.

Questions to ask Speaker 1	Information from Speaker 1
How was your summer?	
Did you go away?	
What stay in a hotel?	
Who did you stay with?	
Did you have a good time?	
What did you do?	
What else did you do?	

2. Here is information about YOUR summer. You will give this information to Speaker 1 when she or he asks you questions. You will sometimes need to add the words *Yes* and *No.*

My summer was pretty good.
I didn't go away. I stayed home because I had to work.
On weekends, I often went to the beach with my family.
We had a great time.
We had barbecues and watched a lot of movies.
I'm happy to stay home.
There are plenty of things to do at home, so I don't need to go away.

Lesson 7, Page 132

For Speaker 1 (Seller)

You like selling old things at a flea market every weekend. Here is information about what you are selling. You will give this information to Speaker 2 when she or he asks you questions. If the shopper thinks your prices are too high (expensive), then you can "bargain." Sometimes you can sell something for a lower price, and sometimes you will not change your price. You decide.

Example of a conversation:

SHOPPER: How much do you want for these plates?

SELLER: They're $10 each. They're very old.

SHOPPER: Will you take $8? (*Or:* How about $8?)

Before you start, write the name of each item on small pieces of paper or on 3" x 5" cards. On the back of the cards, write your prices. Put these cards on your desk so the shopper can see the items, but not the prices.

Items	Prices You Want to Get
very old plates	$10 each
a lamp	$25
a wooden table	$35
a beautiful pitcher	$15
a silver picture frame	$12
sunglasses	$10

When you finish, give the shopper what she or he bought (give the cards).

Lesson 7, Page 132

For Speaker 2 (Shopper)

You just moved into a new apartment and you need many things. You are shopping at a flea market because you can find many interesting and unusual things there, and the prices are cheaper than in most stores.

One seller has many old and beautiful things to sell. You ask, "How much is this?" or "How much are these?" (*OR:* "How much do you want for this/these?") When she or he tells you the price, you can say, "That is too expensive" and then you can ask, "Will you take $___?" or "How about $___?" In other words, you can "bargain." But if you really want something, you can pay what the seller wants.

Example of a conversation:

SHOPPER: How much do you want for these plates?

SELLER: They're $10 each. They're very old.

SHOPPER: Will you take $8? (*Or:* How about $8?)

Here is a list of things the seller is trying to sell at the flea market:

Items	Prices You Want to Get
very old plates	$5 each
a lamp	$15
a wooden table	$28
a beautiful pitcher	$9
a silver picture frame	$7
sunglasses	$5
___________	___________

When you finish, take what you bought (the cards) and thank the seller.

Appendix C: How to Make a Speech

Prepare a five minute speech about a topic that your teacher approves. Suggested topics appear at the end of each lesson. *Additional topics:* my job, a holiday in my native country, how to cook something.

Questions you might ask

1. How will I know if my speech will be five minutes?

    The answer is: by practicing it out loud at home, even if you have to go into a room and close the door.

2. Can I read my speech?

    No. You will need to put short notes (not sentences) on note cards. (But you can write the first and last sentence on a card.) If you use more than one note card, number your cards.

3. How should I start and end my speech?

    To start, say "Today I'm going to talk about _____."
    To end, say "Thank you. Are there any questions?" (Don't end with "That's all.")

4. Can I memorize my speech?

    No. If you memorize your speech, it will sound like you are reading it. It is better to just look at notes and then make your own sentences.

5. How can I practice?

    - Find a quiet place.

    - Record your speech if you can.

    - Practice more than once.

    - Time your speech.

6. Can I change my topic?

    If you change your approved topic, you should talk to your teacher to make sure that your new topic is OK.

7. How will I be evaluated?

    Your teacher and two of your classmates will complete an evaluation form. You will also complete a self-evaluation. The three evaluation forms appear on pages 179–181.

Sample note card for speech

(You will probably need more than one card.)

Introductory Sentence: Today I'm going to talk about my job.

- my job interview
- when I got the job
- the people at work:
  - my boss
  - my friends
- my hours at work and what I do:

  -
  -
  -

Conclusion: summary + the kind of job I want in the future

Concluding Sentence: Thank you. Are there any questions?

SPEECH EVALUATION BY TEACHER

Name of Speaker: _____ Grade: _____

	Disagree Strongly				Agree Strongly
1. The main idea was clearly stated.	I	2	3	4	5
2. Enough details were given to clarify the main idea.	I	2	3	4	5
3. The speech was well organized.	I	2	3	4	5
4. The speech was well prepared.	I	2	3	4	5

The speaker:

5. showed interest in the topic.	I	2	3	4	5
6. glanced at brief notes and didn't read a written speech.	I	2	3	4	5
7. spoke clearly, at a moderate speed.	I	2	3	4	5
8. spoke in a voice that was neither too loud nor too soft.	I	2	3	4	5
9. recognized when it was necessary to define words and/or give an example.	I	2	3	4	5
10. used visual aids as necessary.	I	2	3	4	5
11. used eye contact effectively—that is, looked at people in all parts of the room.	I	2	3	4	5
12. used humor and smiled when appropriate.	I	2	3	4	5

Pronunciation Notes   **Grammar/Vocabulary Notes**

_____   _____

_____   _____

Comments

_____

_____

_____

_____

SPEECH EVALUATION BY CLASSMATE

Name of Speaker: _____ **Name of Peer Evaluator:** _____

NOTE: Each speech should have at least two peer evaluators.

	Disagree Strongly				Agree Strongly
1. The main idea was clearly stated	1	2	3	4	5
2. Enough details were given to clarify the main idea.	1	2	3	4	5
3. The speech was well organized.	1	2	3	4	5
4. The speech was well prepared.	1	2	3	4	5

The speaker:

5. showed interest in the topic.	1	2	3	4	5
6. glanced at brief notes and didn't read a written speech.	1	2	3	4	5
7. spoke clearly, at a moderate speed.	1	2	3	4	5
8. spoke in a voice that was neither too loud nor too soft.	1	2	3	4	5
9. recognized when it was necessary to define words and/or give an example.	1	2	3	4	5
10. used visual aids as necessary.	1	2	3	4	5
11. used eye contact effectively—that is, looked at people in all parts of the room.	1	2	3	4	5
12. used humor and smiled when appropriate.	1	2	3	4	5

I recommend that next time you _____

_____

_____

One thing very good about your speech was _____

_____

_____

SPEECH SELF-EVALUATION

Name: _____

NOTE: Do this evaluation after watching the recording of your speech, if possible.

		Disagree Strongly				**Agree Strongly**
1.	The main idea was clearly stated.	1	2	3	4	5
2.	I gave enough details to clarify the main idea.	1	2	3	4	5
3.	My speech was well organized.	1	2	3	4	5
4.	My speech was well prepared.	1	2	3	4	5
5.	I showed interest in the topic.	1	2	3	4	5
6.	I glanced at brief notes and didn't read a written speech.	1	2	3	4	5
7.	I spoke clearly, at a moderate speed.	1	2	3	4	5
8.	I spoke in a voice that was neither too loud nor too soft.	1	2	3	4	5
9.	I recognized when it was necessary to define words and/or give an example.	1	2	3	4	5
10.	I used visual aids as necessary.	1	2	3	4	5
11.	I used eye contact effectively. That is, I looked at people in all parts of the room.	1	2	3	4	5
12.	I used humor and smiled when appropriate.	1	2	3	4	5

If I could make this speech again, I would _____

_____

What I especially liked about my speech was _____

_____

Additional comments _____

_____

Appendix D: Hot Seat

Choose one student to come to the "Hot Seat" (a chair) in the front of the room. Or, get into groups and choose one student in each group to be on the "Hot Seat." This student will answer questions. If someone asks a personal question, the student on the hot seat does not have to answer.

When you ask questions, remember to think about question intonation (see Lesson 6).

Possible questions

- What's your name?
- Where are you from?
- Where do you live now?
- Why do you want to learn English?
- Do you like the United States? (Canada, Japan, etc.?) Why or why not?
- What do you do in your free time?
- Do you like to go to the movies? What kind of movies do you like?
- What is your favorite kind of music?
- What is your favorite kind of food?
- Other:

"Taboo" Questions: (Don't ask these because they are too personal.)

Are you married?

How old are you?

What is your religion?

How much money do you make?

How much rent do you pay?

If someone asks you these questions and you don't want to answer, you can answer with a question. For example:

Student A: How old are you?
Student B: How old are YOU?

Or, you can just say, "That's a personal question."

Appendix E: Classroom Language

These are questions and directions that students and teachers often use.
Add to these lists as you, your classmates, and teacher talk in class.

Questions that students often ask in class

1. How do you spell _____?

2. How do you pronounce _____?

3. What does _____ mean?

4. What is the meaning of _____?

5. What is the definition of _____?

6. _____

7. _____

8. _____

Requests that students often make in class

1. Could you please write that on the board?

2. Could you please repeat that?

3. Could you please say that again?

4. Could you please say that more slowly?

5. _____

6. _____

7. _____

Questions that teachers often ask to see if students understand

1. Do you understand?

2. Are you following me?

3. Got it?

4. _____

5. _____

6. _____

Directions that teachers often give students

1. Pass your papers up.

2. Pass these papers back.

3. Hand in (turn in) your homework.

4. Get into groups.

5. Work with a partner.

6. Check your homework.

7. Take turns.

8. _____

9. _____

10. _____

Appendix F: Vowels and Consonants

Vowel Chart

A, E, I, O and *U* are vowels. They are LETTERS of the alphabet. But in English, there are 16 vowel SOUNDS. Look at the chart below.

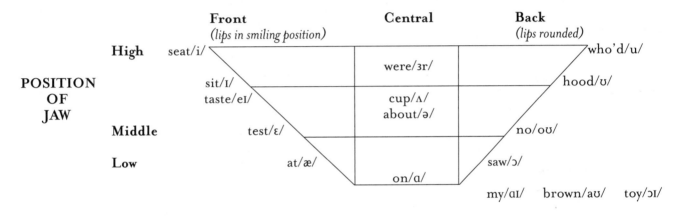

LOCATION OF TONGUE

Consonant Chart

Letters	Sounds	Voiced	Voiceless	Example
b	/b/	x		**b**ut
c	/k/, /s/		x	**c**omputer, s**c**ience
d	/d/	x		**d**inosaur
f	/f/		x	**f**orget
g	/g/, /ʤ/	x		for**g**et, technolo**g**y
h	/h/		x	**h**ome
j	/ʤ/	x		**j**udge
k	/k/		x	thin**k**
l	/l/	x		mai**l**
m	/m/	x		progra**m**
n	/n/	x		wo**n**
p	/p/		x	com**p**uter
q	/kw/		x	**q**uite
r	/r/	x		**r**eally
s	/s/, /z/, /ʒ/	x	x	u**s**, i**s**, u**s**ual
t	/t/		x	grea**t**
v	/v/	x		**v**ery
w	/w/	x		**w**on
x	/ks/		x	si**x**
y	/y/	x		**y**ou
z	/z/	x		**z**oo
ch	/tʃ/, /ʃ/, /k/		x	**ch**ange, ma**ch**ine, te**ch**nology
sh	/ʃ/		x	**sh**e
th	/ð/, /θ/	x	x	**th**is, **th**ink
ng	/ŋ/	x		thi**ng**

Guide to Pronunciation Symbols

Vowels			**Consonants**		
Symbol	**Key word**	**Pronunciation**	**Symbol**	**Key word**	**Pronunciation**
/ɑ/	hot	/hɑt/	/b/	boy	/bɔɪ/
	far	/fɑr/	/d/	day	/deɪ/
/æ/	cat	/kæt/	/ʤ/	just	/ʤʌst/
/aɪ/	fine	/faɪn/	/f/	face	/feɪs/
/aʊ/	house	/haʊs/	/g/	get	/gɛt/
/ɛ/	bed	/bɛd/	/h/	hat	/hæt/
/eɪ/	name	/neɪm/	/k/	car	/kɑr/
/i/	need	/nid/	/l/	light	/laɪt/
/ɪ/	sit	/sɪt/	/m/	my	/maɪ/
/oʊ/	go	/goʊ/	/n/	nine	/naɪn/
/ʊ/	book	/bʊk/	/ŋ/	sing	/sɪŋ/
/u/	boot	/but/	/p/	pen	/pɛn/
/ɔ/	dog	/dɔg/	/r/	right	/raɪt/
	four	/fɔr/	/s/	see	/si/
/ɔɪ/	toy	/tɔɪ/	/t/	tea	/ti/
/ʌ/	cup	/kʌp/	/tʃ/	cheap	/tʃip/
/ɛr/	bird	/bɛrd/	/v/	vote	/voʊt/
/ə/	about	/əˈbaʊt/	/w/	west	/wɛst/
	after	/ˈæftər/	/y/	yes	/yɛs/
			/z/	zoo	/zu/
			/ð/	they	/ðeɪ/
			/θ/	think	/θɪŋk/
			/ʃ/	shoe	/ʃu/
			/ʒ/	vision	/ˈvɪʒən/

Source: The Newbury House Dictionary of American English

Appendix G: Study Tips

1. Study Cards

Buy a set of index cards. On each card, write the following with the expressions that you find most difficult to remember from each lesson.

Expression:

Sentence:

Grammar reminder:

Pronunciation reminder:

Example study card

Expression:	get out of bed
Sentence:	It is hard for me to get out of bed early in the morning.
Grammar reminder:	remember "of"
Pronunciation reminder:	Some people say "owda" for "out of."

2. Cover Your Walls

Do you ever wash dishes? Why don't you hang a card with expressions that you need to study near your sink? You can review while you wash dishes.

Of course, you can hang up cards all over your home. Soon you will be dreaming about expressions in English.

3. Other Ideas

(a) Write new expressions from in or out of class in a small book that fits in a pocket or purse. Study these expressions while you wait for a bus, wait to see a doctor, etc.

(b) Study with others. What are some of the ways you can study together?

_____

_____

_____

(c) Your Suggestions?

_____

_____

_____

Appendix H: Expression Clusters

Every time you finish a lesson, add expressions to the "clusters" below. There are extra lines, so you can add other expressions that you talk about in class. Over time, you will see how many expressions with the same words you have learned. (Write complete expressions on one line.)

Review Game: Using a dark marking pen, write the following words on sheets of paper (one word on each sheet). (Word List: *make, do, take, have, get, go, up, out, down, in, to, of, at*) Students should stand in front of the classroom, each holding a sheet of paper so that everyone can see.

The other students should have index cards with expressions minus the words in the above list. Each student should walk up to and stand by the student who is holding the word that will complete the expression. After everyone is standing in the right place, the groups of students clustered around each word can go to the board and make sentences with the expressions that they form.

Expressions with Verbs

_____   a reservation

_____ (MAKE) _____

_____   _____

_____   (HAVE)   _____

_____   _____

a shower/a bath   _____

_____ (TAKE) _____

_____   _____

_____   (GET)   _____

_____   _____

_____   _____

_____ (BE) _____

_____   _____

_____   (GO)   _____

_____   _____

_____   _____

_____ (DO) _____

_____   _____

Expressions with Helping Verbs

do/does/don't
doesn't/can/can't

_____   _____

_____   _____

_____   _____

Expressions with Small Words

_____   _____

_____ (TO) _____

_____   _____

_____   _____

_____ (ON) _____

_____   _____

_____   _____

_____ (UP) _____

_____   _____

_____   _____

_____ (OUT) _____

_____   _____

_____   _____

_____ (FOR) _____

_____   _____

_____   _____

_____ (BACK) _____

_____   _____

_____   _____

_____ (ABOUT) _____

_____   _____

_____   _____

_____ (AT) _____

_____   _____

_____   _____

_____ (OFF) _____

_____   _____

_____ _____
_____ (DOWN) _____
_____ _____

_____ _____
_____ (IN) _____
_____ _____

_____ _____
_____ (OF) _____
_____ _____

_____ _____
_____ (OTHER) _____
_____ _____

_____ _____
_____ (OTHER SMALL WORDS) _____
_____ _____

Name (Optional): _____ **Date:** _____

Circle the number that shows how much you agree or disagree with the sentences on the left.

		No		Yes
1.	I know many more expressions in English.	1	2	3
2.	Sometimes I try to use some of these expressions when I speak.	1	2	3
3.	When I listen to native speakers of English, I sometimes hear expressions that I studied.	1	2	3
4.	When I see or hear expressions that I don't know, I write them down and ask what they mean.	1	2	3
5.	I know more about pronunciation in English.	1	2	3
6.	I try to think about pronunciation when I talk.	1	2	3
7.	I listen carefully to how native speakers of English pronounce words.	1	2	3
8.	I'm working hard both in and out of class.	1	2	3
9.	I like to work with other students in class.	1	2	3
10.	I like to study with other students outside of class.	1	2	3

Questions/Comments? _____

_____

Where are you in our class?

What number or numbers apply to you? Why?

_____

_____

_____

_____

_____

_____

Expressions from *All Clear 1* That Students Hear Or Read Outside of Class

Outside of class, you will hear and read many of the expressions that you are studying because the expressions are so common.

When you hear or read any of these expressions, write them down on an index card. This will help make you a more careful listener and reader, and you will find that you remember the expressions better.

It would be a good idea if perhaps once a week students in your class shared their lists.

EXPRESSION COLLECTION 1

Sentence with *All Clear 1* expression that I heard or read: _____

_____

_____

Where I heard or read it: _____

_____

_____

Who was speaking: _____

_____

_____

New Expressions That Students Hear Or Read Outside of Class

Outside of class, you will hear and read many expressions in English. You will find them on TV and on the radio, in the movies, on T-shirts, on bumper stickers, and in advertisements. They are everywhere.

Start a collection of these expressions by writing them down on index cards. You can find out what the expressions mean either by asking someone outside of class or by asking your teacher.

It would be a good idea if perhaps once a week students in your class shared their lists.

EXPRESSION COLLECTION 2

Expression/Meaning/Sample Sentence: _____
_____
_____

Where I heard or read it: _____
_____
_____

Who was speaking: _____
_____
_____

Lesson Answer Key

Lesson Answer Key includes

- As You Listen
- After You Listen
- Your Turn Listening Challenge answers and scripts
- Exercises 1, 2, 3, 4 and 10

Lesson 1

As You Listen

- He's worried about starting a new class. He's always nervous on the first day of school. And he's afraid of talking in front of a lot of people.
- Andrea says that he's not the only one who is nervous. She tells him not to worry, and that he will get to know people and make friends.

After You Listen

(A) T, F, ?, T, ?

Your Turn: Listening Challenge

1, 6, 7, 5, 4, 2, 3

Script
A: Hi. Where are you from?
B: Japan. How about you?
A: I'm from Mexico.
B: When did you come to the United States?
A: Oh, about a month ago. And you?
B: About six months ago.
A: Do you like it here?
B: Now I do. But I didn't like it at the beginning.
A: Why not?
B: Hmm . . . well, I didn't understand anything. Everyone was speaking very fast.
A: I know what you mean. Uh . . . You know, I don't know your name . . .
B: It's Rika. What's your name?
A: José. It's nice to meet you.
B: Nice to meet you, too.

Exercises

1. Mini-dialogues

   1 A/B: d, b, e, g, f, c, a

2. Grammar practice

   I.a. took   I.d. had   I.g. got
   I.b. had to   I.e. was   I.h. didn't get
   I.c. didn't have to   I.f. weren't   I.i. made

   2.a. with   2.c. about   2.e. with
   2.b. of   2.d. of   2.f. with

   3.a. flying   3.c. understanding
   3.b. studying   3.d. speaking

3. Error correction

   1. He's taking an English <u>class</u>.
   2. Last year I <u>took</u> a swimming class.
   3. <u>What's</u> wrong with her? She looks very unhappy.
   4. He <u>has</u> to go home after school every day.
   5. They had to <u>go</u> home early yesterday.
   6. I'm not afraid <u>of</u> speaking English.
   7. Are you afraid of <u>speaking</u> English?
   8. We are worried <u>about</u> our next test.
   9. At <u>the</u> beginning of the story, everyone was happy.
   10. At the end <u>of</u> the story, everyone was sad.
   11. Don't worry. You will <u>make</u> many new friends at your school.
   12. You don't have trouble <u>speaking</u> English.

4. Listen and write the expressions

   1. What's wrong
   2. I'm afraid of
   3. have to
   4. Don't worry
   5. make friends
   6. At the beginning
   7. were afraid
   8. get to know
   9. have trouble
   10. are taking
   11. get better

10. Word search

1. What's wrong?
2. At the beginning . . .
3. At the end . . .
4. have trouble
5. get better
6. make friends
7. have to
8. take a class
9. get to know
10. Don't worry about . . . !
11. Are you worried about . . . ?

```
N  I  P  M  H  G  D  J  H  S  R  M  J  B  Y
Y  H  V  C  A  E  L  E  A  D  D  B  T  E  D
Z  W  F  Q  B  T  Q  J  V  N  Y  D  U  G  S
J  W  B  H  H  B  I  F  E  E  G  O  O  N  V
K  Z  V  A  J  E  C  X  T  I  G  N  B  O  U
X  K  L  V  Q  T  V  O  R  R  E  T  A  R  T
D  N  E  E  H  T  T  A  O  F  T  W  D  W  A
T  I  Y  T  H  E  U  W  U  E  T  O  E  S  K
Z  Q  Z  O  V  R  P  O  B  K  O  R  I  T  E
J  G  J  F  T  K  O  W  L  A  K  R  R  A  A
C  N  L  V  E  M  T  I  E  M  N  Y  R  H  C
V  L  M  B  P  U  R  R  P  Y  O  I  O  W  L
J  B  F  T  G  G  D  A  R  C  W  L  W  Y  A
A  T  T  H  E  B  E  G  I  N  N  I  N  G  S
Y  G  R  R  B  E  A  F  R  A  I  D  O  F  S
```

As You Listen

- Alex is calling because he wants to ask Sara to go to the movies with him.
- Yes, Sara wants to see Alex. She can't see him Friday night, but she can see him on Saturday.

After You Listen

(A) 1. Yes, he is.
2. Yes, she is.
3. Yes, he does.
4. No, he doesn't.
5. No, she can't.
6. Yes, she can.
7. Yes, he is.
8. No, she isn't.
9. Yes, they are.

Your Turn: Listening Challenge

c, f, d, a, e, b

Script
1. It's a nice day.
2. We have a test tomorrow.
3. I want to learn how to play the guitar.
4. I'm tired.
5. They're bored.
6. We're hungry.

Exercises

1. Mini-dialogues

   1 A/B: e, a, f, b, c, d

2. Grammar practice

1.a. held/hung	2.a. on	3.a. I'll
1.b. couldn't	2.b. for	3.b. don't
1.c. got	2.c. off	3.c. can't
		3.d. there's
		3.e. it's
		3.f. Who's

3. Error correction

1. <u>I'll</u> be right there.
2. A: Hello.
   B: Hi. Can I please speak to Katie?
   A: <u>Who's this</u>?
3. A: Hello.
   B: Hi. Is Katie there?
   B: Yes, <u>hold on</u>.
4. Hello. <u>This is</u> Steve. Can I speak to Mike?
5. Wait! Don't hang <u>up</u>! I want to speak to Mom, too!
6. My hands are wet. Can you <u>get</u> the phone?
7. I'm sorry. I can't make <u>it</u> on Monday, but I can be there on Tuesday.
8. Why <u>don't we</u> have coffee after class?
9. They picked <u>me up</u> in front of my house.
10. A: I'm late because I was in traffic for two hours.
    B: That <u>sounds</u> terrible!
11. Sorry. I need to get <u>off</u> the phone because it's time for dinner.
12. Julie—<u>It's</u> for you!

4. Listen and write the expressions

1. Who's this
2. This is
3. Hold on
4. It's for you
5. I'll be right there
6. Why don't
7. That sounds
8. pick you up
9. hang up

10. Unscramble and find the secret message

LOHD NO   H | O | L | D   O | N
              (2) (9)

GANH PU   H | A | N | G   U | P
                    (7)

HOW'S GCLLAIN   W | H | O | ' | S   C | A | L | L | I | N | G | ?
                         (5)   (14)

CPIK PU   P | I | C | K   U | P

EGT FFO   G | E | T   O | F | F
               (13)

HOW'S SITH   W | H | O | ' | S   T | H | I | S | ?
                       (10)

THSI SI   T | H | I | S   I | S
              (4)

TI'S FOR OYU!   I | T | ' | S   F | O | R   Y | O | U | !
                          (6)

I'LL BE HGRTI HEETR.   I | ' | L | L   B | E   R | I | G | H | T   T | H | E | R | E | .
                                   (11)

CAN'T MEKA IT   C | A | N | ' | T   M | A | K | E   I | T
                     (8)

SRWANE HET HEOPN   A | N | S | W | E | R   T | H | E   P | H | O | N | E
               (3)   (12) (15)

WHY NOD'T   W | H | Y   D | O | N | ' | T
                          (1)

T | H | A | T   S | O | U | N | D | S   G | R | E | A | T | !
(1) (2) (3) (4)   (5) (6) (7) (8) (9) (10)   (11) (12) (13) (14) (15)

Lesson 3

As You Listen

- They're going to go to the beach.
- It's winter now.

After You Listen

(A)   F, T, F, ?, F

Your Turn: Listening Challenge

1. It's his wedding anniversary and he wants to take his wife out to dinner.
2. His wife.
3. By the window.
4. Saturday night at eight o'clock.

Script

A: Ruby's Place. May I help you?
B: Yes. I'd like to make a reservation for two for Saturday night.
A: What time?
B: Eight o'clock?
A: OK. And your name please?
B: Healy. H - E - A - L - Y.
A: OK. That will be Saturday night at 8:00 for two.
B: Right. And can I reserve a table by the window? It's our wedding anniversary and . . .
A: No problem.
B: Thanks a lot. See you on Saturday.
A: Bye.

Exercises

1. Mini-dialogues

   1 A/B: d, b, g, e, c, f, a

2. Grammar practice

1.a. went	2.a. for	3.a. a
1.b. took	2.b. on/to	3.b. an
1.c. was	2.c. on	3.c. a
1.d. didn't have/had	2.d. for	3.d. a
1.e. went/didn't go	2.e. of	3.e. A
1.f. wasn't	2.f. for/for	
1.g. made	2.g. of	

3. Error correction

1. We went for a <u>walk</u> yesterday.
2. It's a beautiful day. Let's go for <u>a</u> walk.
3. They took a <u>walk</u> yesterday.
4. They go shopping every Saturday morning.
5. Our teacher gives us plenty <u>of</u> homework.
6. The party <u>is</u> very crowded. Let's go home.

7. There are a lot <u>of</u> people at the party.
8. There is lots <u>of</u> good food at the party.
9. There are plenty <u>of</u> drinks at the party.
10. I called the restaurant and <u>made</u> a reservation for four people.
11. The store is closed. They are <u>on</u> vacation for two weeks.
12. They go on <u>a</u> trip to San Francisco every year.

4. Listen and write the expressions

1. go away
2. go swimming
3. took long walks
4. plenty of
5. wasn't crowded
6. what else
7. went dancing
8. went ice skating

Lesson 4

As You Listen

- He needs to get up because he has to go to the airport.
- He's having trouble getting up because he went to bed late last night, and now it's very early and cold and dark.

After You Listen

(A) T, ?, F, ?, T

Your Turn: Listening Challenge

1. Wake up! You're late!
2. Don't fall asleep again! Get up!
3. Don't go back to sleep! Get out of bed!
4. Get dressed! You're late!
5. Put on a jacket! It's cold!

Script

1. Wake up! You're late!
2. Don't fall asleep again! Get up!
3. Don't go back to sleep! Get out of bed!
4. Get dressed! You're late!
5. Put on a jacket! It's cold!

Exercises

1. Mini-dialogues

   1 A/B: d, g, i, c, h, f, a, b, e

2. Grammar practice

1.a. went/woke
1.b. fell
1.c. slept
1.d. got
1.e. took
1.f. put

2.a. to
2.b. of
2.c. for
2.d. on
2.e. off

3.a. me/you/him/her/us/them (or a name)
3.b. them
3.c. shoes/jacket, etc.
3.d. shoes/jacket, etc.
3.e. shoes, jacket, etc.

4.a. help
4.b. me/coffee/lunch, etc.
4.c. money/time
4.d. buy/get

3. Error correction

1. Mike <u>woke</u> up after Tom went to the airport.
2. Mike took <u>a</u> shower and got dressed before he had breakfast.
3. He put <u>on</u> warm clothes because it's cold today.
4. Every day he goes to work at 12:00. So he always has time <u>to</u> read the newspaper in the morning.
5. When he gets home from work, he <u>takes</u> off his work clothes and puts on blue jeans.
6. A: Does he wear blue jeans?
   B: Yes, he puts <u>them on</u> after he gets home from work.
7. Last night, he <u>went</u> to sleep late, so he's tired today.
8. Last night, he <u>fell</u> asleep at 3:00 a.m.!
9. He needs to <u>sleep</u> more.
10. He always goes <u>to bed</u> late.
11. When he sleeps <u>late</u>, he's late for work.
12. He's very busy. His girlfriend says he has no time <u>for</u> her.

4. Listen and write the expressions

1. get up
2. went back to sleep
3. woke up
4. had time
5. put on
6. took a shower
7. got dressed
8. need to

10. Unscramble and find the secret message

TKOO A ERHSWO   T O O K | A | S H O W E R

26   29   28 38   39 50 3

TOKO A RTPI   T O O K | A | T R I P

35   16 48

OKOT FFO   T O O K | O F F

18

NWTE TO PESLE   W E N T | T O | S L E E P

17

TWNE CKAB OT LSEPE   W E N T | B A C K | T O | S L E E P

45   31   4

ELFL SLEAPE   F E L L | A S L E E P

15

LTESP AELT   S L E P T | L A T E

36   42 11

EYDTSA PU   S T A Y E D | U P

22   2   5   40

TGO TOU OF DEB   G O T | O U T | O F | B E D

8

TGO PU   G O T | U P

19 6

GTO RSDESDE   G O T | D R E S S E D

20 9 49

DNEEED OT   N E E D E D | T O

32 23 27 46 34   7

ADH EIMT TO   H A D | T I M E | T O

33 25 13   37 21 24 1   43

HDA IETM RFO   H A D | T I M E | F O R

44 41 10   30

UPT NO   P U T | O N

12

OWEK UP   W O K E | U P

47   14

E A R L Y | T O | B E D | A N D | E A R L Y | T O | R I S E

1 2 3 4 5   6 7   8 9 10   11 12 13   14 15 16 17   18 19   20 21 22 23

M A K E S | A | M A N | H E A L T H Y , | W E A L T H Y , | A N D

24 25 26 27 28   29   30 31 32   33 34 35 36 37 38   39 40 41 42 43 44   45 46

W I S E .

47 48 49 50

As You Listen

- They are celebrating the sister's birthday.
- Her brother is going to pay.

After You Listen

(A) 1. a
2. b
3. b
4. b
5. a

Your Turn: Listening Challenge

b, c, a, c, b

Script

1. Where do you want to have lunch?
2. When do you want to study for the test?
3. Do you want me to bring dessert or salad to your party?
4. When do you want to go to the city?
5. Where do you want to sit?

Exercises

1. Mini-dialogues

   1 A/B: b, e, f, g, a, d, c   **2 A/B:** e, a, d, b, f, g, c

2. Grammar practice

1.a. ate
1.b. didn't eat
1.c. went
1.d. didn't go

2.a. to
2.b. in
2.c. for

3.a. It's
3.b. I'd/We'd
3.c. I'm/We're
3.d. She'll/He'll and I'll
3.e. I'm/He's/She's/You're/We're/They're

3. Error correction

1. We eat out once <u>in</u> a while.
2. We didn't <u>eat</u> out last night.
3. I <u>am</u> thirsty.
4. I can't believe it. They <u>treated</u> me to dinner last week.
5. They go out <u>to</u> eat every Wednesday. It's expensive!
6. A: Are you ready to order?
   B: Yes, <u>I'll</u> have the chicken.
7. A: Will that be all?
   B: Yes, <u>that's</u> all.

4. Listen and write the expressions

1. eat out
2. treat
3. Can I take your order
4. whatever you want
5. am very hungry
6. I'd like
7. I'll have
8. We're ready to order
9. What would you like
10. I'll have
11. Will that be all
12. for now

10. Word search

1. wherever you want
2. are thirsty
3. ate outside
4. go out to eat
5. for now
6. that's it
7. ready to order
8. I'll have
9. We'd like

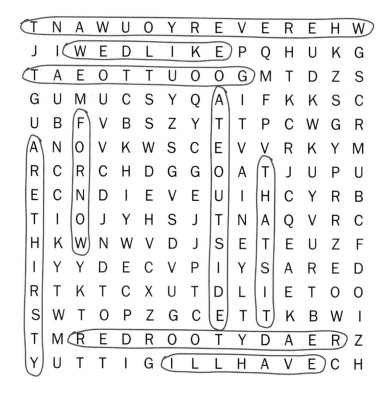

As You Listen

- He fell down because we went down the stairs too fast.
- She's going to call an ambulance.

After You Listen

(A) 1. Yes, he did.
2. Yes, it does.
3. No, it doesn't.
4. No, he doesn't.
5. Yes, he can.
6. Yes, she is.
7. Yes, they are.

Your Turn: Listening Challenge

1. take aspirin
2. drink tea
3. go to the dentist
4. do back exercises
5. go to the doctor

Script
1. My head hurts.
2. My stomach hurts.
3. My tooth hurts.
4. My back hurts.
5. My ear hurts.

Exercises

1. Mini-dialogues

   1 A/B: e, a, d, b, c, e   **2 A/B:** a, d, c, b, e

2. Grammar practice

1.a. fell

1.b. hurt

1.c. didn't hurt

2.a. of

2.b. off

2.c. down

3.a. What's happening?

3.b. What happened?

3.c. I think so. *OR:* I don't think so.

3.d. Stay put/be right back.

3. Error correction

1. I lost my dictionary. I think it fell out <u>of</u> my backpack.

2. Be careful. Your glass is going to fall <u>off</u> the table.

3. The shelf in my closet is completely full. When I opened the door, everything on the shelf <u>fell</u> down.

4. Stay put. I will <u>be</u> right back.

5. His knee is <u>getting</u> swollen. He needs some ice.

6. A: Why is she walking like that?
   B: She <u>hurt</u> her back yesterday.

4. Listen and write the expressions

1. is killing me

2. What happened

3. fell down

4. is swollen

5. right away

6. I'll be right back

7. I think so

Lesson 7

As You Listen

- They ask her about the price of the jeans, and if Jim can try them on.
- Yes, he does.

After You Listen

(A) ?, T, T, F, ?

Your Turn: Listening Challenge

1. it   3. it   5. them
2. them   4. it

Script
1. This is a nice suit.
2. Those look like warm gloves.
3. This shirt is too small.
4. I love your hat.
5. These shorts are OK.

Exercises

1. Mini-dialogues

    1 A/B: g, c, d, e, b, a, f, h

2. Grammar practice

1.a. try them on
1.b. try them on
1.c. try it on
1.d. trying on
1.e. tried on

2.a. these
2.b. these
2.c. this
2.d. these
2.e. this

3.a. are they
3.b. is it

3. Error correction

1. It's 3:30. I need to <u>go</u> home right away.
2. I <u>go</u> to school at 9:00 every morning.
3. When I <u>go</u> back to my native country, I will see my family.
4. These shoes are really comfortable. I'll take <u>them</u>.
5. I just got new glasses. What do you think <u>of</u> them?
6. I like your glasses. Can I try <u>them on</u>?
7. I didn't try the jeans <u>on</u>, and now I have to return them.
8. How <u>do</u> these glasses look on me?
9. How does this shirt <u>look</u> on me?
10. Thanks. <u>We're</u> just looking.
11. How much <u>is this</u>?
12. How much <u>are</u> these? *OR:* How much is <u>this</u>?

4. Listen and write the expressions

1. we're just looking
2. Let me know
3. What do you think of
4. How much is it
5. try this on
6. over there
7. go on in
8. How does this look
9. We'll take it

10. Unscramble and find the secret message

ROEV EETRH

O	V	E	R		T	H	E	R	E

(4 under V)

CEMO ON IN.

C	O	M	E		O	N		I	N	.

(11 under I)

I'LL AKTE TEHES NSJEA.

| I | ' | L | L | | T | A | K | E | | T | H | E | S | E | | J | E | A | N | S | . |

(10 under second L)

TWAH OD YOU ITNKH OF SHTI?

| W | H | A | T | | D | O | | Y | O | U | | T | H | I | N | K | | O | F | | T | H | I | S | ? |

(12 under O)

EW'RE UJST LIKGONO.

| W | E | ' | R | E | | J | U | S | T | | L | O | O | K | I | N | G | . |

(1 under K)

I ETDRI HTEM NO.

| I | | T | R | I | E | D | | T | H | E | M | | O | N | . |

(5 under I)

GO ON NI.

| G | O | | O | N | | I | N | . |

(8 under I)

TLE EM KNOW.

| L | E | T | | M | E | | K | N | O | W | . |

(9 under L)

WOH CMHU ARE THYE?

| H | O | W | | M | U | C | H | | A | R | E | | T | H | E | Y | ? |

(3 under H, 14 under W, 13 under A, 15 under R)

OWH UCHM IS STHI?

| H | O | W | | M | U | C | H | | I | S | | T | H | I | S | ? |

(7 under T)

WOH OD HYET OLKO?

| H | O | W | | D | O | | T | H | E | Y | | L | O | O | K | ? |

(6 under D)

OWH DSEO IT OLOK?

| H | O | W | | D | O | E | S | | I | T | | L | O | O | K | ? |

(16 under D, 2 under I)

I		S	H	O	P	P	E	D		T	I	L	L		I		D	R	O	P	P	E	D	!
1		2	3	4		5	6		7	8	9	10	11		12	13	14		15	16

As You Listen

- She's late because she missed her train.
- The husband took a nap.

After You Listen

H, W, H, W, H , H, H

Your Turn: Listening Challenge

_____✓_____ a vacation
_____✓_____ a concert
_____ a TV show
_____✓_____ a grade
_____ a party
_____✓_____ food
_____ a test
_____✓_____ a parent
_____✓_____ a baby
_____ a new car

Script

1. My cousin just had a baby. I can't wait to see him.
2. He's very tired. He can't wait for his vacation.
3. The teacher gave a test yesterday. I can't wait to see my grade.
4. Their concert is next week. I can't wait!
5. I'm so hungry. I can't wait for dinner.
6. The little girl can't wait for her father to come home. She wants to play with him.

Exercises

1. Mini-dialogues

   1 A/B: d, e, a, b, f, c   **2 A/B:** d, f, c, b, a, e

2. Grammar practice

I.a. for
I.b. to
I.c. to
I.d. for
I.e. for

2.a. took
2.b. got
2.c. made
2.d. couldn't
2.e. did, did

3. Error correction

1. The baby is getting <u>sleepy</u>. She needs to take a nap.
2. The baby <u>takes</u> a nap every afternoon.
3. I took <u>a</u> nap for twenty minutes, and now I feel better.
4. We need to be at the theater in time for the beginning of the movie.
5. We need to be at the theater in time to see the beginning of the movie.
6. He <u>does</u> his laundry once a week.
7. I <u>did</u> the dishes last night. Can you do the dishes tonight?
8. They <u>got</u> home late last night.
9. She can't wait to see you.
10. She can't wait for her birthday party.

4. Listen and write the expressions

1. did the laundry
2. the dishes
3. get back
4. in time to
5. No problem
6. get home
7. make sure
8. can't wait
9. getting sleepy
10. take a nap

10. Word search

1. taking a nap
2. got back
3. got home
4. make sure
5. getting sleepy
6. do the dishes
7. on time
8. in time to
9. in time for
10. can't wait for
11. can't wait to
12. miss the bus

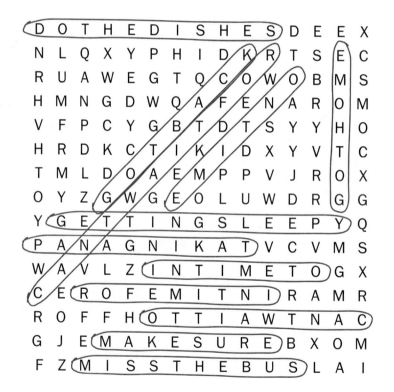

Review Answer Key

Lessons 1 and 2

1. get better
2. get off the phone
3. get to know someone
4. worry about
5. That sounds great!
6. at the beginning
7. at the end
8. What's wrong?
9. I'll be right there.
10. take an English class
11. Who's this?
12. Who's calling?
13. be afraid of
14. hold on
15. have trouble speaking
16. have to do something
17. pick up
18. It's for you.
19. can't make it
20. make friends
21. hang up

Lessons 3 and 4

1. take off your sweater
2. take a trip
3. take a shower
4. take a bath
5. take a walk
6. take a vacation
7. go on a trip
8. go away
9. go to bed
10. go back to sleep
11. make a reservation
12. get dressed
13. get up
14. get out of bed
15. have time for
16. Have a good trip!
17. put on your coat
18. fall asleep
19. wake up
20. a lot of
21. What else?
22. plenty of
23. be crowded
24. be on vacation

Lessons 5 and 6

1. for now
2. fall off the table
3. fall out of his pocket
4. fall down
5. I don't think so.
6. once in a while
7. What would you like?
8. Will that be all?
9. It's my treat!
10. go out to eat
11. Are you ready to order?
12. whenever you want
13. Is that it?
14. stay put
15. eat out
16. right away
17. It hurts.
18. We're ready to order.
19. be thirsty
20. I'll be right back.

Lessons 7 and 8

1. No problem!
2. I hope not!
3. I'll take it.
4. try on
5. get home
6. get sleepy
7. do the laundry
8. take a nap
9. We're just looking.
10. Let me know.
11. What do you think of this?
12. Can you wait over there?
13. How much is this?
14. Come on in!
15. I can't wait to see you.
16. I can't wait for the weekend.
17. miss the plane
18. get back at 7:30
19. in time to go to my class
20. in time for my class
21. get to school on time
22. Make sure you do your homework.

Crossword Puzzle Solutions

Lessons 1 and 2

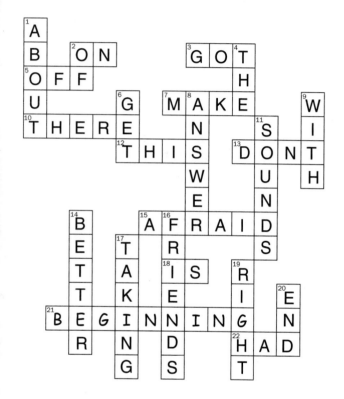

Lessons 3 and 4

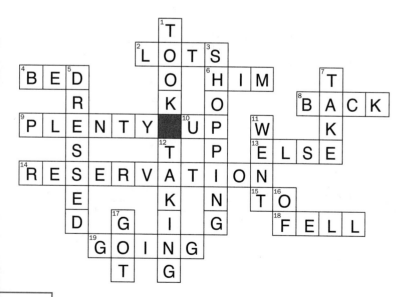

Crossword Puzzle Solutions

Lessons 5 and 6

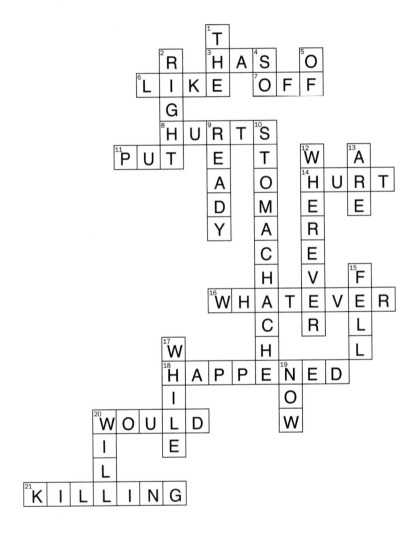

Crossword Puzzle Solutions

Lessons 7 and 8

Index: Alphabetical List of Expressions

The purple number refers to the lesson number(s). The black number refers to the page number.

S

T

W